Advanced Fashion Drawing
Lifestyle Illustration

Bil Donovan

Advanced Fashion Drawing
Lifestyle Illustration

Laurence King Publishing

LAURENCE KING

Published in 2010 by Laurence King Publishing Ltd
361–373 City Road
London EC1V 1LR
Tel: +44 20 7841 6900
Fax: +44 20 7841 6910
Email: enquiries@laurenceking.com
www.laurenceking.com

This book was designed and produced by Laurence King
Publishing Ltd, London.

A catalog record for this book is available from the British Library.

ISBN: 978 1 85669 648 7

Designed by Studio Ten and a Half

Printed in China

Front cover: Bil Donovan, *Lady in Red* (detail), 2007. Ink and watercolor.
Back cover: Bil Donovan, *Plaid-Chic*, 2008. Gouache.
Frontispiece: Bil Donovan, *Lounge Girls*, 2006. Gouache.

Contents

Related study material is available
on the Laurence King website at
www.laurenceking.com.

DONOVAN

Preface and Acknowledgments

Anyone can learn to draw. Just as anyone can throw a ball, pirouette, or play a violin, anyone can make a drawing. For some, it is natural; for others, lacking natural skill, it's a labor of love motivated by passion. I assumed I was of the former variety until, in my first semester at the Fashion Institute of Technology, New York, I was informed by a professor that I was of the latter and should rethink my artistic pursuit.

Drawing fashion had been a passion of mine since childhood and I asked what I could do to remain in the Fashion Illustration program. "Draw!" was the reply. "You will need to draw, draw, and draw. Draw everything, anything, anytime, or anyplace, just draw it."

And I did.

I began to fill sketchbook after sketchbook with drawings. I drew my friends, my apartment, my laundromat; I drew my cat, my hat, and faces on the bus or train. I drew from photos, memory, and ideas, but mainly I drew from life. Drawing from life is challenging and nurtures a better sense of draftsmanship and observation skills.

I got better.

My drawings improved to the extent that the very same professor, astonished at my progress, commended me by nominating me for an award. That professor, Rosemary Torres, became a friend and put me on the right path to honing my skills. Encouraged, I started taking additional classes at the Philadelphia College of Art (now the Art Institute of Philadelphia), the Fashion Institute of Technology, the School of Visual Arts, Parsons School of Art and Design, and the Art Students League.

I loved the energy and environment of drawing studios, with a circle of artists at easels surrounding a model stand. I spent many years as a student in these environments with many extraordinary teachers.

Jack Potter introduced a series of premises usually involving shape as a backdrop for drawing. Barbara Pearlman's classes were characterized by the opera music blaring from the stereo that infiltrated the drawings through a line that was emotional yet concise. Ana Ishikawa balanced both shape and line in figures that were grounded through anatomy and diagonals. Steven Meisel charged the room with energy; Jane Bixby Weller slowed it down with knowledge and calculated charm. Peter Hristoff broke the rules and Judy Mannarino reinvented them. Each instructor's style inspired and challenged the artist through a variety of ideas revolving around one theme: drawing the figure.

When I became a teacher, I wanted to motivate, inspire, and challenge my students as those instructors had me. Teaching presented the challenge of how to communicate my experiences, ideas, and exercises into a fifteen-week semester.

I started by incorporating Jack Potter's formula of weekly premises, which I defined as visual words forming a vocabulary for drawing. I forwarded this idea with exercises that not only simplified the figure in terms of line and shape, but incorporated texture, value, and chance against a backdrop of composition.

My first realization was that consistency was important in order to communicate a different set of ideas each week. That consistency came in the shape of the figure, literally. I now use this shape—the figure—as a template to investigate the weekly exercises.

My next realization was that throughout the fifteen-week semester, the skills that the exercises provided to the students went far beyond the scope of a course in fashion drawing or illustration; these were tools or words in a visual vocabulary that would serve the students in many creative disciplines outside of the class as well.

Sometimes life comes full circle, and the opportunity to present this information to a wider audience occurred in the same hallway where I was once told that I should rethink my major. An esteemed colleague and friend, Professor Karen Santry, presented me with the opportunity of writing this book.

And I did.

Acknowledgments

I am indebted to the generosity of those artists who gave permission to allow their work to be reprinted, and to my colleagues at the Fashion Institute of Technology, especially Karen Santry, who presented me with this opportunity and challenge, Karen Cannell, Head of Special Collections, who procured the images from the Frances Neady Collection, and Kristen Rock and Rocío Cintrón, who assisted in archiving, scanning, and formatting those images.

I've been fortunate to work with Laurence King Publishing, and thank all of my taskmasters who are now valued friends: Laurence King, for his patience and support in allowing me to shape this book; Lee Ripley, my publishing editor, a visionary with a sharp eye and style, who was the first to recognize the uniqueness and significance of this book; my editor, Anne Townley, who shares my passion and enabled that passion and my voice to surface through the written word; my managing editor, John Jervis, who was responsible for bringing this book to completion; Claire Murphy, who relentlessly sought and procured the guest art work. Also, a special mention to Charlie Bolton and Angus Hyland, who translated the information into a simple yet sophisticated format that creates a striking and beautiful backdrop that illuminates the information.

Most importantly, my partner, Ken Nintzel, who was unwavering in his support and faith in the mission of the book.

Above all, this book is my homage to the artists, teachers, and students who have inspired me; it is my attempt to share the magic.

Opposite: In this brush and ink image for Christian Dior Beauty, *Petals*, I used a number of the drawing premises found in this book: line, shape, value, composition. Working in today's lifestyle illustration market not only demands technical knowledge, but also constant practice: drawing, experimenting, challenging yourself, and challenging the rules.

Below: This illustration, *Man in Black*, demonstrates that the traditional skills explored throughout this book—observation, utilizing shape and line, and the principles of composition—are invaluable. They are also essential in the application of digital programs —in this case, I used Photoshop and Illustrator.

Introduction

This book is unique.

The exercises are geared toward illustrators with the intention of simplifying the principles and ideas that are associated with the genre of fashion illustration and the lifestyle market. Although the figure is initially used as a template to examine these principles and ideas, this book is not only about drawing the traditional fashion illustration figure. There are no systematic charts of nine or ten heads to measure a typical first croquis. The focus is not on how to draw a collar or cuff, or render fur or satin, or draw an eye. The idea is not to reinforce a particular method of drawing. Instead, the exercises in the book challenge the student to reinvent their notions of looking and drawing and to analyze the visual of the figure in terms of line, shape, and value.

This book is geared toward the advanced student who has a working knowledge of the figure and drawing. However, the information provided will be of use to anyone at any level, as the exercises promote observation and draftsmanship. Structured around the method of using weekly sessions to expand the visual vocabulary of students, the book is primarily about the possibilities of drawing the figure and capturing a lifestyle.

Lifestyle illustration can seem an elusive term that defies definition. "Lifestyle" reflects the style of dress, environment, entertainment, consumption, and social habits of a culture. Illustrations that visually capture the essence of the lifestyle of a segment of society are, therefore, defined as lifestyle illustration. Advertising and promotional campaigns are geared toward such targeted audiences; the role of the illustrator working in this market is to create an illustration that not only reflects a particular lifestyle but also is attractive to the audience. This can be achieved by incorporating a fashion sensibility into an illustration, whether it is of a fashion show, luxury hotel suite, cruise ship, cocktail glass, or urban skateboarders.

The aim of this book is to provide the artist with the tools to transform the most mundane of settings into a stylized and graphic visual. In addition, because the exercises focus on thinking and choice, the information is not limited to a lifestyle market; they can as easily be applied to the genres of caricature, graphic novels, and general illustration as well.

How the Exercises Work

The exercises are structured in a simple format to nurture draftsmanship, sharpen drawing skills, and incorporate composition into the equation.

The book begins with the slow methodical drawing process that I refer to as the balancing act. This fosters a solid observational skill, which in turn nurtures the draftsmanship of the student. The next exercise, breaking the figure into simple contour lines, reinvents the figure as a template for composition.

Composition is the main backdrop upon which the exercises in shape and line quality perform. The ability to see the figure in terms of shapes allows for a quick rationalization of the visual, which can then be translated through line, value, and technique. Exercises in line quality simplify this elusive concept and introduce the student to a simple process of incorporating line quality into an illustration. They also demonstrate how to use the idea of line quality to indicate depth and space on the figure.

Throughout all the exercises, selectivity challenges the student to think, before drawing a line or placing a shape within the figure, about how that line or shape will affect the whole of the figure—much like analyzing the layout of a framed space to apply the principles of composition.

All of the exercises in this book nurture the concept of composition. The student, using the premises of selectivity, contrasting shapes, and negative space from the first half of the book, will already be acquainted with some of the terms and principles of composition in layout and design that are promoted in the second half of the book.

Here, using the principles of composition—perspective, symmetry, the rule of thirds, scale, positive and negative space, repetition and pattern, value and color—the student will begin to create a finished illustration that reflects the lifestyle market.

To complete that illustration, the student will also learn how to explore and use a wide range of media, from brush and ink to collage and Photoshop, in the second half of the book.

The world of illustration and art is organic and constantly evolving to reflect trends and changes in the marketplace. To meet the needs of that market, an illustrator needs not only to find his or her own style, but also to feel comfortable with changing and reinventing that style. Suggestions for finding a style and then breaking the rules in order to explore new avenues form the closing discussion in the book. It is my hope that this will inspire and motivate those who are as passionate about drawing as I am.

Chapter One
Line

A line is a line is a line. In the act of drawing, perhaps no other component or factor is as valuable in shaping and communicating depth, life, energy, and personality as a line.

A line can be rigid or fluid. It can have weight and presence or be delicate and seem to float translucently beneath the surface of the paper. It can be quick or studious, continuous, rhythmic, or aloof. Line can be all or a combination of these characteristics.

The personality of a line can be used to define leather or chiffon, create a texture to mimic reptile goods, capture the movement in a skirt, or with one stroke illustrate the arch of an eyebrow.

We will explore the personality of line in Chapter 4. Here we will begin with the basic contour line. Integrity of line will be examined through a balancing act; exercises incorporating straight, curved, and opposition of line will be included to allow the student to acquire a basic foundation for seeing and communicating the figure.

The Contour Line

The contour line creates a solid outline of the image; it is very different to a rapidly executed sketch. It will be used to discover and realize the silhouette of the figure.

Integrity of Line

There are numerous ways to observe and draw the figure. The method applied in this book uses a balancing method. In this method you will draw the figure in stages, starting from the left side, then moving to the right, and then back to the left, and so on down the figure using various points on the model to anchor your line. This exercise is most successful if done very slowly, maintaining the integrity of the line, not allowing one side of the drawing to extend too far below the other, much like the balancing movement of a seesaw. It is important to balance the length of line from one side of the figure to the other, allowing yourself time to observe distance, proportions, and the angles of the figure.

1.1 The Balancing Act

Preparation

For this exercise, the following supplies are necessary:

One pad of 18 x 24in (A2) white all-purpose
paper or comparable

Charcoal pencils—hard to medium

Kneaded eraser

Ideally, this lesson should be done with a live model. Although
the same results can be achieved with the use of a photo, it is to
your benefit to accustom yourself to drawing from life rather than
photos. Drawing from life is more challenging and is a proven
method of training your eye to communicate three-dimensional
form in a drawing. Photos are usually distorted, so a drawing from
a photo of a fashion model will seem squat and out of proportion.

Ask a friend, acquaintance, or family member to pose for a series
of positions. If this is not an option, you could use any bottle that
has some unusual curved and straight lines in its shape, such as
a wine bottle or perfume decanter, an accessory such as a shoe,
a pair of sunglasses, or a handbag—and of course, there is always
the option of drawing yourself in a mirror.

To prepare, you will need the supplies listed and a surface to
work upon. The live model or the selected photo should be simple
in dress, pose, and nature. If a photo is your only option then
this reference should be posted on a surface directly in front
of you rather than placed beside the drawing pad. This will allow
you to observe from a distance and mimic the idea of a live model
who would be posing in a similar position in relation to your
drawing surface.

We begin the initial drawing using a charcoal pencil on a pad of
18 x 24in (A2) all-purpose paper that has been turned horizontally.

Note:
It is important with each drawing of the
figure that you make while carrying out
the exercises in this book that you place
the head at the top of the horizontal paper.
This allows you to begin to get a sense of
proportion. The consistency of this placement
will encourage you to think about size and
how to fit the whole figure into the space
on the paper.

1.1 The Balancing Act

Directions

One technique that will be used throughout most of the chapters in this book is that of drawing from the top of the model's head down to the feet. This is a technique where the eye slowly follows the outside shape of the form and communicates that observation with a contour line. This is an important tool in developing a good sense of draftsmanship.

Step One

Beginning from the center point of the head, slowly observe the slant of the head, noting the slant of the diagonal. Begin to draw a strong contour line from the center point to the left side of the head, anchoring that line to the top of the ear (see Figure 1).

Step Two

Once accomplished, return to the top of the center point of the head and begin to follow the shape of the right side of the head and anchor this line to the top of the right ear, observing as you continue which ear is higher or lower than the other (see Figure 2).

Step Three

Return to the left side and continue from the ear to the base of the neck or shoulders. Then balance this line on the other side, comparing which side of the neck or shoulder is higher and which is lower (see Figure 3).

Step Four

Once the shoulder lines are balanced, follow through to an area that is distinctly higher or angular in nature, such as the elbow or waist or top of the hip, again comparing which of these anchor points is higher or lower than the same point of the body on the opposite side (see Figure 4).

Follow this method, continuing to allow gravity to drag your line down the figure and constantly making pit stops to observe, compare, and make adjustments, until you have drawn the contour shape of the complete figure (see Figures 5–8).

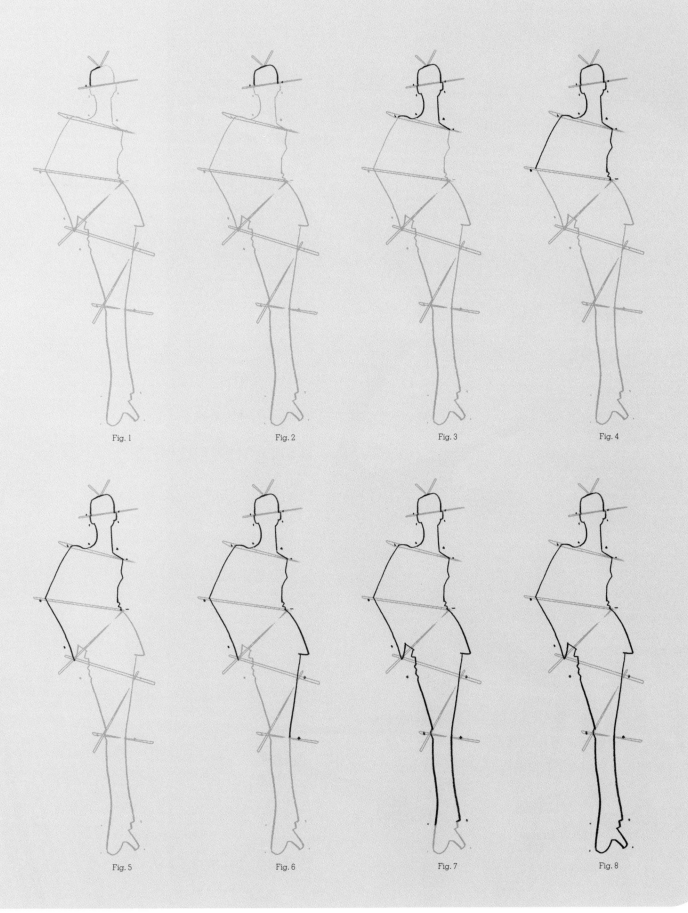

Fig. 1   Fig. 2   Fig. 3   Fig. 4

Fig. 5   Fig. 6   Fig. 7   Fig. 8

14

1.2 Straight Line

Imagine that you are given the task of communicating the figure in a language of strictly straight lines. The terms "curve," "round," and "fluid" do not exist in this language. Now entertain the idea that you will draw this figure with your charcoal as if you were using a ruler to accomplish the task. If you did use a ruler, this challenge would soon become very tedious. Having to draw every fold in the garment or every loose hair on the head would eventually cause you to try to limit the number of lines you used, forcing you to become more selective. Use this idea of selectivity to accomplish this drawing. The aim is to make yourself focus and find the line that best communicates the image.

Preparation

For this exercise, the following supplies are necessary:

One pad of 18 x 24in (A2) white all-purpose paper or comparable

Charcoal pencils—hard to medium

Kneaded eraser

The pose used for this exercise has negative space visible between the arms, which, unlike the solid shape created by the balancing-act outline, will be represented in the final drawing.

In this and the following two exercises, you will be drawing a single figure using a straight line, a curved line, and a combination of the two. The purpose of these exercises will be more apparent if you see the resulting three figures side-by-side on the paper, so start this first straight-line drawing on the left-hand side of an 18 x 24in (A2) piece of paper, pinned horizontally to your drawing surface. Position the top of the head of this figure near the upper left-hand side of the pad and close to the edge of the paper to sustain consistency in proportion.

Negative Space:
After you have drawn a line around all the positive shapes you see in front of you, the areas left behind are called negative space.

Note:
It is important at this stage that you draw with a dark, deliberate line. The pressure you use when making your line will reinforce a slow, observant method. The balancing-act technique will encourage you to notice the diagonals, verticals, and horizontals in the figure. It allows for an understanding of measurement and observation of high and low points in the figure that will serve as a guide for your drawing.

1.2 Straight Line

Directions

Now that you are acquainted with the balancing-act method, it is time to apply this technique to the exercises.

In this instance, again start at the top of the head of the figure, continuing to utilize the balancing act to guide the straight-line contour drawing. Continue to draw the whole figure. Once completed, draw and define the negative shapes within the contour drawing.

Step One

Beginning from the center point of the head, as you did in the balancing act, slowly observe the slant of the head, noting the slant of the diagonal. Use a straight line to draw to the left and then to the right. Continue with straight lines, and, noting the balance points, continue down to the shoulder line—an obvious straight line in the figure (see Figure 1).

Step Two

As you contine to draw down the arms, you will see how the tubular shape lends itself to the use of straight lines, but choose your lines carefully when you come to draw the curve of the arm around the elbow (see Figure 2).

Step Three

You will find more straight lines in the legs as you continue down the body, but will have to use selectivity to communicate the curves around the shoes (see Figure 3).

Step Four

Finally, look for areas of negative space between the arms and the body and outline these using straight lines to define the shape of the figure (see Figure 4).

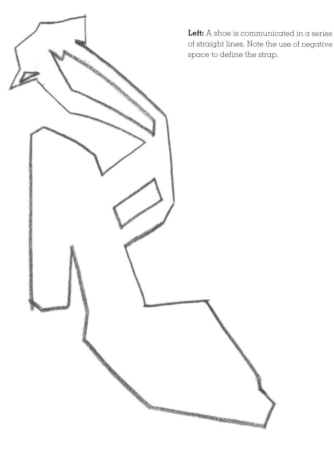

Left: A shoe is communicated in a series of straight lines. Note the use of negative space to define the strap.

16

Fig. 1

Fig. 2

Fig. 3

Fig. 4

Below: Understanding the difference between straight and curved lines and how to play on that difference can be a useful tool in creating interest in a simple two-color illustration. Here, the contrast between the straight lines used to convey the keyboard player and the curvaceous lines used to portray the singer could not be greater. The selectivity in contrasting the lines accentuates the singer, lends character to the performers, and brings a sense of dynamism to this illustration, *Jazz Band Rouge*, by John Jay Cabuay.

1.3 **Curved Line**

Now that you have mastered the language of straight lines to create a contour drawing, the following exercise will introduce a new language: the curved line.

This time, imagine that the only line that exists in your vocabulary is a curved line. Employing the balancing act once again, you will communicate a contour outline drawing with rounded and curved lines. In order to achieve this, visualize the figure as an inflated balloon. Most balloons have no sharp, angular edges. Round, soft, or tubular in nature, an inflated balloon will enlarge and exaggerate the character of the deflated balloon. This is the effect you are trying to achieve. You will find in this exercise that you will make greater exaggerations than in the straight-line exercise.

In the previous exercise you will have found that some areas of the figure were naturally straight and, therefore, easy to communicate with straight lines. In this drawing you will discover areas of the figure that are intrinsically curvaceous and easy to communicate with a curved line. Your challenge is not only to exaggerate these areas but also to interpret any angular areas into rounded lines.

Preparation

For this exercise, the following supplies are necessary:

One pad of 18 x 24in (A2) white all-purpose paper or comparable

Charcoal pencils—hard to medium

Kneaded eraser

You can continue to draw your friend in the same pose as you did for the straight-line exercise or continue to draw the same accessory, or use a new pose. Place this drawing in the center of your piece of paper, to the right of your straight-line drawing.

20

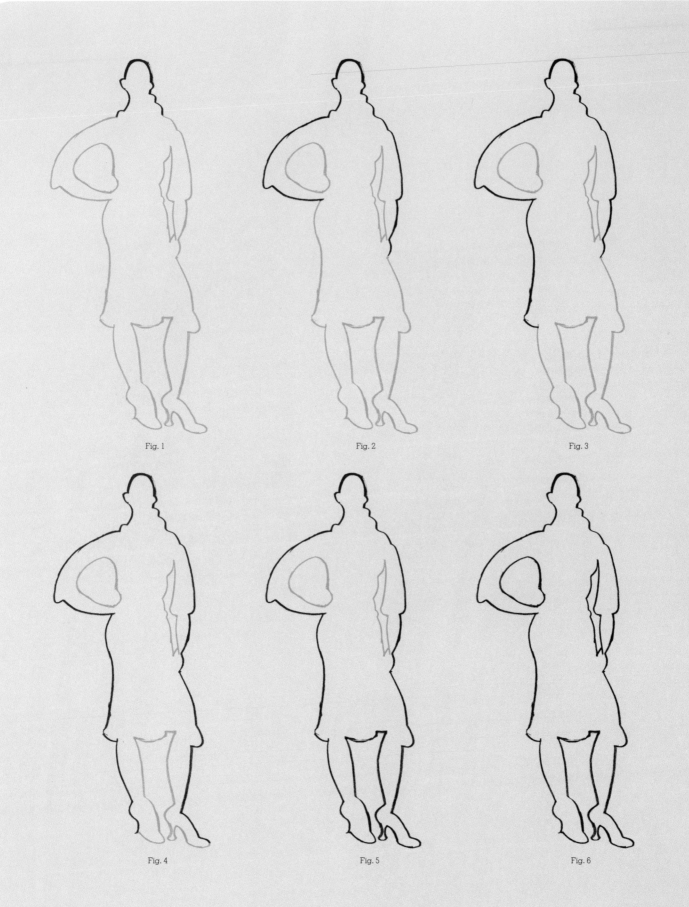

Fig. 1

Fig. 2

Fig. 3

Fig. 4

Fig. 5

Fig. 6

1.3 Curved Line

Directions

Observe before drawing, think about the shape of the figure that is guiding your line, select the line, and exaggerate the curves to communicate what you see. Your finished drawing will be exaggerated.

Step One

Beginning from the center point of the head, ignore any straight lines you might find in the figure and use only rounded lines as you draw your line down first the left and then the right-hand side of the head and shoulders (see Figure 1).

Step Two

You will find that the arms seemed easier to convey using straight lines. Here they will look more like a rubber doll (see Figure 2).

Step Three

Contine to draw your line down the figure, using the balancing act. By using curved lines you can convey more of a swing to the skirt (see Figure 3).

Step Four

Once again, the legs, which could more accurately be portrayed using straight lines, will look a little rubbery (see Figure 4).

Step Five

Complete the figure using curved lines to convey the shoes (see Figure 5).

Step Six

Finally, draw in the areas of negative space, this time using curved lines (see Figure 6). Your figure will look much more exaggerated than the one you drew using straight lines.

Left: Compare this shoe, conveyed in curved lines, with that composed from straight lines on p. 16. This shoe seems to have an entirely different form, especially around the toe.

Below: Argentinian illustrator, Pablo Lobato, created this image of the Tuvan throat-singing ensemble, Huun-Huur-Tu, for *The New Yorker*. In contrast to the previous illustrations, where the use of straight and curved lines was not as pronounced, Pablo pushes the premise of straight and curved line to its extreme. The figures, costumes, and instruments are geometric in nature and balanced in a rhythmic composition that conveys energy and movement.

22

1.4 Combination of Straight and Curved Lines

Having completed the previous two exercises, it should be obvious that restricting a drawing exclusively to straight or curved lines is problematic in communicating the figure properly. The exercise of using straight lines made you realize that some areas of the figure are curved, and vice versa when utilizing the curved line.

That is exactly the idea. These exercises force you to focus on the silhouette of the figure and while doing so observe and break down the figure in a simple terminology of straight and curved lines. In the following exercise, you will combine these two ideas to communicate the figure in a strict combination of curved and straight lines.

I emphasize the term "strict," as in this series of drawings you will continue to observe which areas of the figure work better if drawn with straight lines, and which work best with curved; use those characters of line strictly for each area, without merging the two.

Preparation

For this exercise, the following supplies are necessary:

One pad of 18 x 24in (A2) white all-purpose paper or comparable

Charcoal pencils—hard to medium

Kneaded eraser

Place this third image on the right-hand side of your piece of paper. You can continue to use the same pose or accessory or work with a new pose.

1.4 Combination of Straight and Curved Lines

Directions

It is important to first observe, second analyze, and third select the correct line to communicate what you see. The finished drawing should be exaggerated, with a visible difference between the straight and curved lines, and cartoon-like in nature.

Step One

Again starting at the center point of the head and using the balancing act, draw the line down, first down the left and then the right-hand side of the figure.

Step Two

As you work, look for the areas best communicated with a straight line and those areas best communicated with a curved one and use both appropriately. You will have a good idea from your previous two drawings where to use each kind of line. Incorporate exaggeration to emphasize the contours of the figure.

Step Three

Complete the drawing by adding in any areas of negative space.

Left: A combination of straight and curved lines conveys the character of the shoe.

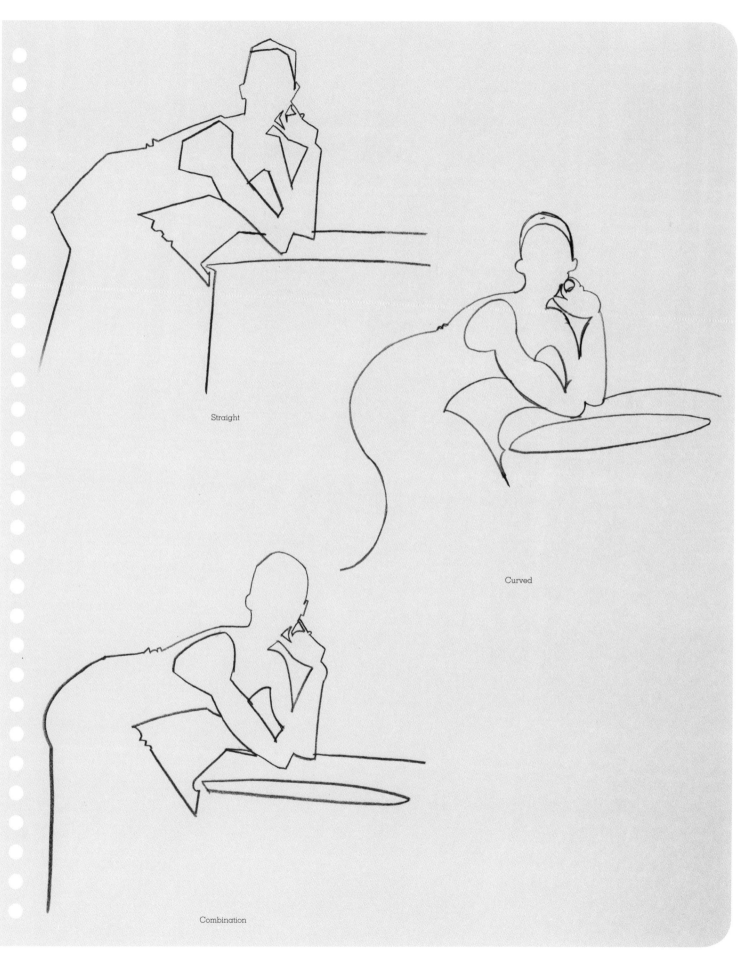

Straight

Curved

Combination

Assignment

Draw three frames in your sketchbook. Into these frames, you will
do three self-portraits from the top of your head to your shoulders.
Think about composition and how you would like to position the
portraits into the frame and how they will occupy the space. Areas
of the portraits may be cropped to make an interesting composition.
Draw one portrait in straight lines, another with curved, then
a combination of both straight and curved. Include facial features
and any details of clothing that are visible.

Straight   Curved   Combination

Illustrations by Irvin Rodriguez

Straight   Curved   Combination

Illustrations by Elena Ambotaite

1.5 **Opposition of Line**

Opposites Attract. Period. Behind this premise is the idea that one does not exist fully without the other. Think black without white, warm without cool, or straight without curves. The specific characteristics of each of these pairs of elements when contrasted tend to accentuate each other as complements. Now that you have understood the idea of communicating the figure in a combination of straight and curved lines, it is time to utilize this exercise and push it further.

Observation is key in communicating a drawing that has integrity and gravitas and one that will be compelling to the viewer. Using the balancing-act method of slowly observing the figure will guarantee that you take notice of the differences between the right and left side of the figure and nurture a drawing built on integrity. Now we will move one step further and think about those differences, learning how to push and pull them, creating exaggeration. Exaggeration is another way of contrasting the differences. It will help you to create a more dynamic drawing that is unique to your eye and vision.

To do this, we will use opposition—using opposing characteristics of line and shape on opposite sides of the figure; if one shoulder is higher, then we will make it even higher, while making the opposite one lower. Opposition is a tool you can use to subtly push and pull the various forms, angles, or lines of the visual without creating a drawing that is abstract or grotesque in nature. The finished drawing should reflect the figure or visual, but make it just a bit more dynamic.

Egon Schiele demonstrates opposition of line in his simple line drawing *Three Street Urchins* of 1910 (see right). This drawing, devoid of color or background, is a study in contrasts and as such compelling to observe. Allow your eye to measure the outside contour line of the foreground figure, beginning at the center of the head and moving from the left to the right, making comparisons of Schiele's intent to push and pull the contrasts. Observe the tilt of the head, shape of the scalp, and the difference between the ears. Notice, too, the exaggerated diagonal of the jaw, the lines he uses to describe the neck, collar, shoulders, arms, and pants, as well as the negative space between the arm and the waist. Then take a moment to compare the descriptive contrasts between the foreground and the middle figure and eventually the background figure as well.

Above: Egon Schiele (1890–1918), *Three Street Urchins*, 1910. Pencil on brown paper, 17.6 x 12.1in (44.7 x 30.8cm). Albertina, Vienna

Preparation

For this exercise, the following supplies are necessary:

One pad of 18 x 24in (A2) white all-purpose paper or comparable

Charcoal pencils—hard to medium

Kneaded eraser

1.5 Opposition of Line

Directions

In this exercise, again using the vocabulary of straight and curved lines, you will allow your eye and line to push the diagonals inherent in the figure such as the tilt of the head, shoulders, and hips. You might also incorporate a curved line against a straight line. You can also allow selectivity to place a clean or simple line that conveys a complex area of clothing with a single interpretative line versus an informative line that captures every fold or crease in a garment. Use the negative space created by the pose, such as the space between the arms and legs, to communicate opposition. Creating exaggeration in this way and using your eye to push the premise of opposition will garner further interest in a drawing that at this point is limited to contour line.

Step One

Start from the center point of the head. As you work your way down the figure using the balancing act, look at the diagonals in the figure and think what you can do to incorporate exaggeration in terms of line and form. In the normal drawing shown here (see Figure 1), the head is mainly composed of curved lines. To create opposition and exaggeration (as shown in Figure 2), use a combination of straight and curved lines in opposition and make the tilt of the head more exaggerated.

Step Two

Moving down the figure, observe the slant of the shoulders. Figure 1 shows that there is a slight tilt, with the left shoulder lower and the right higher. The collar also doesn't look particularly furry in texture. In Figure 2, the characteristics of the fur on the collar are exaggerated using straight lines on the left-hand side, while more curved lines on the right-hand side give a less angular quality. At the same time, the collar is used in Figure 2 to exaggerate the angle of the shoulders, pulling the left side even lower and raising the right higher.

Step Three

Now, as you move down to the arms, observe the sleeves. In Figure 1 they are similar in nature. In Figure 2 the forms are exaggerated, narrowing and widening to make a more interesting composition. The shapes of the cuffs are also exaggerated and the difference of the angle of the hands on the hips has been pushed.

Don't forget to observe the negative shapes formed by the space between the arms and the side of the body. In Figure 1, the shapes are similar on the left and the right. In Figure 2, the shapes have been pulled and pushed to create a squarer shape on the left as opposed to a longer, more rectangular shape on the right.

Step Four

Finally, moving down to the hips and the legs, you can exaggerate the line of the hip on the left-hand side versus the right, the shape of the skirt and line of the hem, and the shape of the legs, creating more distance between the legs by pushing the left leg farther into the background.

Fig. 1   Fig. 2

In this illustration, Sirichai has made effective use of exaggerated diagonal and vertical lines and shapes to elongate the figures. Cropping the figures also enhances the impression of height in the image.

30

Chapter Two
Elongating the Figure using Verticals, Horizontals, and Diagonals

The phrase "from head to toe" is appropriate in discussing the verticals, horizontals, and diagonals in the figure. In this chapter you will learn how to recognize these characteristics in the figure and how to use them to enable you to draw a graceful figure over which the eye will move easily. This is an important characteristic of lifestyle illustration, especially when drawing a figure to show clothing to best effect.

In every pose you will find a combination of verticals, horizontals, and diagonals that you can use to stylize and elongate the figure. Most lifestyle and fashion figures are stylized and elongated because this is accepted as the best way to show off the clothes—on the same tall figures that dominate the catwalk. Having said that, in today's lifestyle market all sizes and variations are valid and you may not always have to elongate, or only to a very subtle degree. For this reason, I tend not to follow the rigid nine-, ten-, or twelve-head rule in elongating the figure but instead practice a more fluid method.

The verticals, horizontals, and diagonals inherent in the figure are an important feature to recognize and you will find yourself continually referring to and using them throughout the remainder of the book. In the previous chapter we looked at opposition and at how push and pull could be used to create a more dynamic drawing. There we touched on the idea of using the verticals, horizontals, and diagonals to accomplish this goal. In this chapter we take things further forward; you will learn which lines to accentuate, which to push and pull, and which to use selectively, minimally, or eliminate altogether. You will also find that exaggeration is a key element in elongating and stylizing the figure.

2.1 Verticals

The eye usually observes from head to toe when analyzing a figure. Accentuating the vertical lines allows the eye to move quickly through the figure. This can be used as a tool to elongate and stylize the figure as well as anchoring the figure in a given space. (We will discuss the concept of anchoring the figure in more detail in Chapter 5.)

Elongating the figure is best done by focusing on the areas that allow for elongation naturally: primarily the neck, arms, and legs.

Preparation

For this exercise, the following supplies are necessary:

One pad of 18 x 24in (A2) white all-purpose paper or comparable

Charcoal pencils—hard to medium

Kneaded eraser

Directions

Starting from the head, and using the balancing-act method, begin to draw the figure, accentuating the vertical lines and lightening up on the horizontal lines. Consider using selectivity to communicate the horizontal lines or eliminate them altogether.

As you work your way down the figure, concentrate on pushing the verticals of the neck, arms, and legs to elongate them. To elongate an area, just extend the actual line by ⅛–¼in or by a few millimeters.

When you are drawing from the neck to the shoulders, allow your line to nudge forward a bit depending on the size of your drawing.

Then, using push to exaggerate the length a bit more, do the same with the upper arm as it reaches the elbow and continue with the forearm before it hits the wrist.

From the waist, begin to elongate the hips and continue with the legs.

Elongate accessories such as a scarf. You can also use these to emphasize movement and to add drama.

It will take time for you to develop the habit of elongating the figure, but eventually it will become second nature.

Compare the differences between Figure 1 and Figure 2. The differences are very subtle, but you should notice the following:

Figure 1 is devoid of selectivity. There are many horizontal lines, such as the hair, jawline, and the creases in the fabric at the elbows and knees, and there is no variation between the horizontal and vertical lines. Figure 2, on the other hand, was drawn with selectivity and the idea of accentuating the vertical lines to create a flow through the figure as well as elongating the figure. The importance of the horizontals has been eliminated, while the line of the hair has been pushed and the angle and length of the neck, hips, and legs exaggerated. Opposition has been used to vary the difference between the shoulders and the hemline of the coat and to accentuate movement.

Fig. 1   Fig. 2

34

Fig. 1

Fig. 2

2.2 Horizontals

Think of the movement of the eye as it follows along the shape of a figure composed entirely of horizontal lines as compared to one composed solely of vertical lines. In most cases, the eye will move and flow more rapidly through the figure composed entirely of vertical lines as opposed to one of only horizontal lines. Horizontals that are strong in line and shape break up the figure and tend to arrest the eye and stop the flow of movement.

In this exercise, think how your use of line will allow the eye to move over the surface. Continue to practice selectivity, eliminating the horizontals, leaving only those that can be considered as rest stops or areas that will complement the verticals.

Preparation

For this exercise, the following supplies are necessary:

One pad of 18 x 24in (A2) white all-purpose paper or comparable

Charcoal pencils—hard to medium

Kneaded eraser

Directions

Proceed to communicate the figure in line using the balancing act, as in the vertical exercise.

Focus on selecting and eliminating the horizontals, and use a lighter line for those that you do decide to include.

At the same time, continue to accentuate the lines for the verticals while elongating the figure at the neck, arms, and legs.

Begin to push the diagonals to create a more interesting figure, such as in the slant of the head, the shoulders, arms, waist, and hips.

Use vertical or diagonal fluid lines in the clothing whenever possible to give the figure some movement.

Compare the differences between Figure 1 and Figure 2. Again, you will find these are subtle.

The pose is very straightforward in both Figure 1 and Figure 2, but in Figure 1 the drawing was made without much consideration to observing the verticals and horizontals; the figure looks a bit squat and stiff compared with the exaggerated version in Figure 2.

In Figure 2, opposition was used to select areas of the hairstyle to create a more interesting look. Pushing the slant of the head and lightening up on the features allows for a more attractive face. The neck is also elongated and the diagonals of the scarf are exaggerated. This plays well against the clean lines of the torso. The fold lines at the elbow and wrist have a lighter line quality. The sash at the waist has been angled to complement the diagonals of the shoulders and the diagonal of the hemline has been similarly pushed. The line of the left-hand leg has been exaggerated to complement that of the supporting leg.

2.3 Diagonals

As you have probably noticed at this point, diagonals were incorporated into each of the previous exercises. A diagonal is one of the most important elements to incorporate into a drawing. Using the slants and angles of the figure will make your drawing dynamic and create a flow and movement to allow the eye to revolve around the drawing.

Try exaggerating the diagonals in the slant of the shoulders, arms, waist, and hips. These diagonals allow for an interesting composition and play of opposition and exaggeration within the strict vertical of the figure.

Preparation

For this exercise, the following supplies are necessary:

One pad of 18 x 24in (A2) white all-purpose paper or comparable

Charcoal pencils—hard to medium

Kneaded eraser

Directions

Again using the balancing-act method, focus on finding the diagonals in the figure and exaggerate these angles.

Use the verticals to elongate the figure and be selective when it comes to the horizontals.

Give yourself poetic license to push and pull areas of the figure that would create more exaggerated diagonals or verticals and allow this license to also elongate the figure.

Compare the differences between Figure 1 and Figure 2. Note in Figure 2 the exaggeration of the hair, the angle of the eyebrow that follows the hairline, the shoulders, the pushing of the torso in a more diagonal direction, and the waist, sash, legs, and feet.

Fig. 1   Fig. 2

The apparent simplicity of this watercolor
illustration by Mats Gustafson is, upon closer
observation, revealed to be a selective series
of shapes: the large and small shapes and
dark and light values work together to form
a sublime composition.

Chapter Three
Beginning a Vocabulary of Shapes

I love shapes. Plain and simple. Big or small, busy, clean, textured, patterned, in color value or black or white, silly or serious—shapes rule! Shapes are one of the most important elements in observing and creating visual art. They are the guiding force in layout, design, and composition, whether in drawing, painting, sculpture, or photography, or the creation of a garment. Look around and you will find yourself surrounded by shapes of all sizes, positive as well as negative, composed of light, shadow, texture, and pattern.

We are introduced to shape from an early age and taught to differentiate between a square peg and a round one. Most of us were unconsciously introduced to the language of shapes when we first put crayon to paper and colored inside the lines of a simple illustration in a coloring book. Those contour drawings were made up out of various shapes that together composed a single image. Each shape was closed up with borders to allow us to color inside the line.

Understanding shape, and seeing the world around you in terms of shape, will allow you to break down what you see into simple forms, thus allowing you to draw, paint, or create a dynamic illustration.

In this chapter you will learn how to use shape—or, more correctly, how to incorporate shape into a drawing. You will also have an opportunity to exercise selectivity and communicate your personal style and viewpoint.

Be warned that there will be much examination and discussion of shapes in this chapter, as well as in the chapters to come. You will learn to see and communicate in shapes—it's a great language.

Beginning a Vocabulary of Shapes

Selectivity and Choice

Through simple exercises using line, and thinking about contrasting the differences (opposition), we will deconstruct the figure in terms of shape and use that deconstruction to build a blueprint of the figure. The blueprint is the initial step from which you can build; with a solid foundation to start from, the possibilities are endless. In the previous chapters, we used selectivity to elicit a stronger graphic image. Selectivity will again be a constant companion to the use of shape in this chapter; you will be asked to think first and use your mind more than your drawing medium.

When observing the figure we see a composite of light and value, textures and patterns, colors, lines, and folds. It can seem overwhelming to the untrained eye. Therefore, the exercise of using the balancing act establishes a starting place to begin the drawing. The restrictive practice of using straight and curved lines forced you to analyze the figure—actually the shape of the figure—and break down some of the overwhelming information into simple lines. Chapter 2 offered a guide to seeing the figure in terms of the verticals, horizontals, and diagonals inherent within it while also demonstrating how to push and pull those factors to elongate and create a cleaner image. All of these premises should be incorporated into the following exercises on shape.

Less is More

In this chapter you will again be editing and selecting in your quest to communicate the figure in terms of shape. This might seem straightforward, but the challenge is to identify the shapes that seem to communicate the image best. In composition and graphic art, the simpler the layout and design the greater the impact that image makes. So too with communicating the figure in terms of shapes. The fewer the number of shapes you use the more important those shapes become. Consider the idea of creating a composition where, in a square frame, you have drawn 579 shapes of similar shape and size to fill the entire space. The importance and prominence of the shapes as individual shapes will diminish as you continue to add more into the space. Now take that same space and draw three shapes of varying form and size within it. Each of those shapes now takes on a specific characteristic and becomes unique in its own form, and will complement the other shapes. That is, of course, if there is thought behind the selection of those shapes; without thought and selectivity, filling a space with less could be just that—less. The key here is to observe, think, be smart, select, and develop a drawing that, regardless of the number of shapes it contains, is interesting and dynamic.

Above: In this illustration, Chuck Nitzberg uses the premise of selectivity to compose a face in a series of shapes. Each shape has a distinct character of line, media, or texture. The shapes complement and contrast one another, creating a sense of tension and drama that compels the viewer to take a second glance.

3.1 Drawing the Figure in Three Shapes

I am often asked when directing this exercise if the figure should be drawn in geometric shapes such as circles, squares, or rectangles. The answer is no. The drawing may observe those elements, but should reflect the reality of the figure and not abstract it in geometric forms. When you are attempting to draw and observe the figure, therefore, you will not be exaggerating the figure into a cubistic form.

The key to achieving the desired goal of using shape is observation and thinking. We sometimes rely on what we know rather than what we see: if I asked you to draw an eye from memory, you could; if I asked you to draw a pant leg, I'm sure you could, but your drawings would probably lack depth and integrity as they would have no basis in reality. Drawing what you see rather than what you know, however, will make your drawings far more believable.

The previous chapters explored the figure in simple terms of a contour line and communicated the form of the figure in one shape—the contour line encompassed the entire shape of the figure. Now we will divide the figure into three distinct shapes. In this exercise, negative spaces, such as those between the arms or legs, are not considered to be part of the three shapes.

Preparation

For this exercise, the following supplies are necessary:

One pad of 18 x 24in (A2) white all-purpose paper or comparable

Charcoal pencils—hard to medium

Kneaded eraser

3.1 Drawing the Figure in Three Shapes

Directions

First, have the model take a pose. Spend a minute or two observing the figure before you start drawing, and mentally break up the figure into three shapes. In order to draw the whole figure it will be necessary to combine shapes, since the figure is composed of many different shapes.

Using the balancing act, begin by drawing the figure from the head. Close up each shape before you move on to the next, as if you were creating a simple image for a coloring book. This will allow you to observe, think, and communicate the shape as you proceed through the figure.

Make the drawing interesting and inventive. It would be easy to draw the head as one shape, the torso as another, and then make the bottom of the figure the third shape. That would be expected. Make the viewer work. Do not let them off too easily. Think selectivity!

The illustrations here show that there is no single way of doing this exercise. You can unite different areas of the figure into any one shape. In Figure 1, for example, the head, upper torso, scarf, and arms are drawn in one shape, the rest of the torso and the right leg in another, and the left leg in a third.

Which do you think best communicates the figure? Do you feel that each brings a different perspective to the drawing?

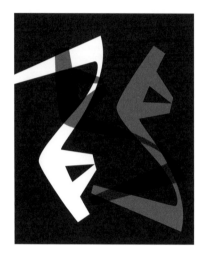

Above: In this illustration of shoes and gloves, Bo Lundberg has repeated a single shape to convey each accessory. His use of negative shapes and line to contrast and define the images adds further interest to the composition.

42

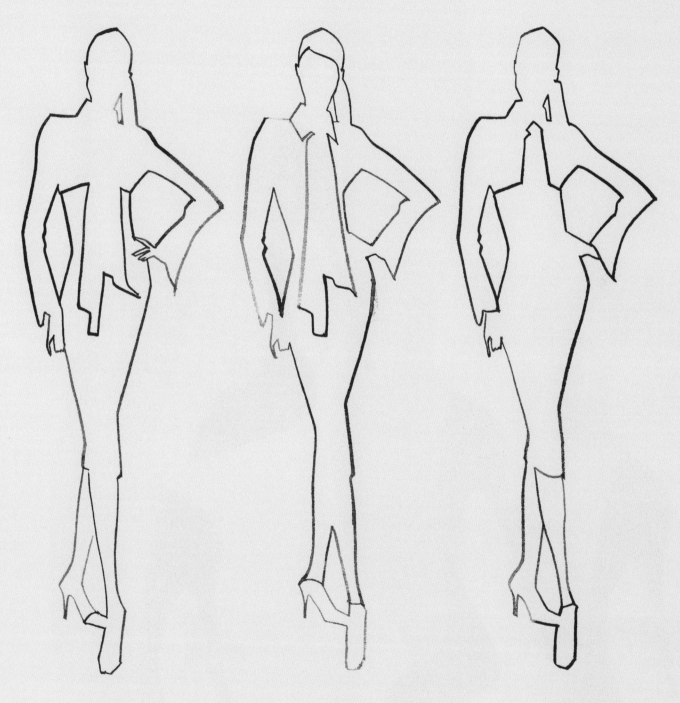

Fig. 1

Fig. 2

Fig. 3

3.2 Drawing the Figure in Five Shapes

After completing the last exercise, your drawings will look edited. Selectivity will have guided your observation and will have resulted in a well-thought-out drawing and composition. Now we will up the ante and communicate the figure in five shapes. Following the same guidelines as in the three-shape exercise, continue to observe, think, and create. This time, if it seems applicable, add the negative shapes as well. You can either add these after all five shapes are complete or as you work through the figure.

Preparation

For this exercise, the following supplies are necessary:

One pad of 18 x 24in (A2) white all-purpose paper or comparable

Charcoal pencils—hard to medium

Kneaded eraser

Opposite: Michael Roberts's witty image, from his book *Fashion Victims*, illustrates the perils of walking in high heels on the sidewalk and is an exercise in the minimal use of shapes. A collage rendered by hand in cut paper, the skillful handling of shape, color, rhythm, and selectivity enhances the movement of the legs and directs attention to the single pink shape in the illustration.

3.2 Drawing the Figure in Five Shapes

Directions

In the same way as in the three-shape exercise, first have the model take a pose. Spend a minute or two observing the figure before you draw, and mentally break up the figure, this time into five shapes.

Using the balancing act, begin by drawing the figure from the head and close up each shape before you move on to the next.

Here Figures 1 and 2 show how you can be even more inventive when using five shapes. Figures 3 and 4 show how using selectivity and adding a few more shapes can bring even more definition to your drawing.

Test Your Skills

Have a model take a pose for five minutes. Examine the figure from head to toe, but do not draw anything; just mentally record what you see. When the five-minute period is over, have the model break, then quickly sketch in line what you remember, taking no more than five minutes.

Then have the model resume the pose and check your drawing against the pose for accuracy. Now repeat this idea with another pose, only this time when you are observing the figure and mentally recording the pose, break the pose up into five to seven shapes. Then draw what you remember in shapes. See if you were able to communicate the pose more correctly by breaking the figure into shapes rather than line.

Fig. 1

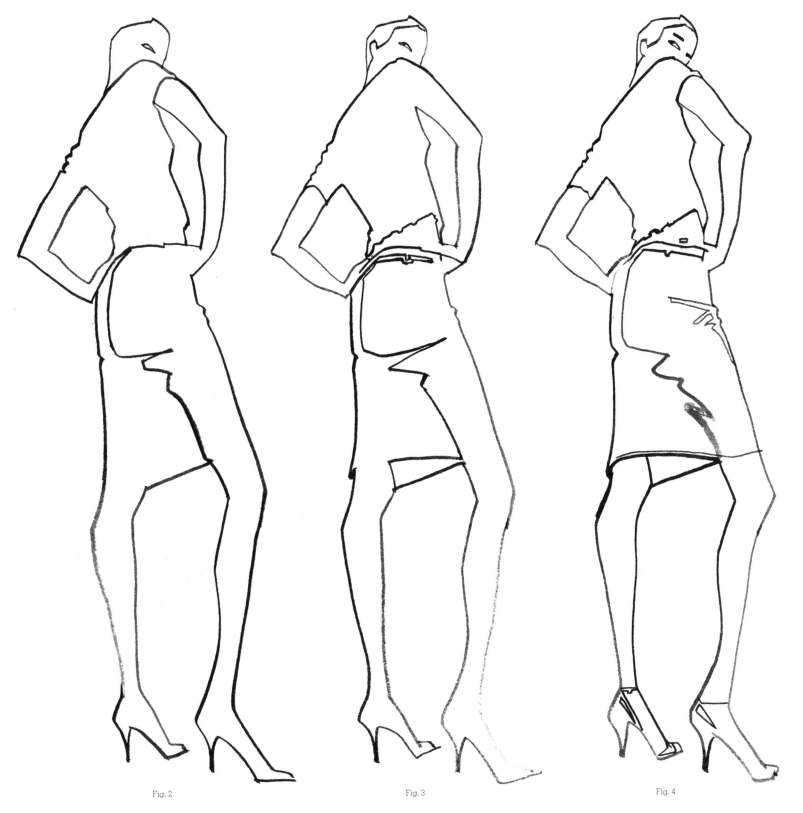

Fig. 2

Fig. 3

Fig. 4

Sonya Suhariyan uses a myriad of shapes to communicate the figure in this illustration. Key shapes are identified with which to compose the figure; each shape is then filled with numerous other shapes and patterns. Even the negative shapes between the arm and the body and behind the figure are filled with pattern and color.

48

3.3 Mapping the Figure

For this exercise, start by thinking about a paint-by-number kit. The line-art image is broken up by a series of shapes; many shapes to be exact. The idea behind mapping the figure in this exercise is based on the same premise. Three, five, seven to hundreds if not thousands of shapes could be used to communicate the figure. In this instance, try breaking up the figure into seven shapes. Once you have completed the seven shapes, choose one of the shapes, go into that shape, and add three to five shapes within it. For instance, if you choose the face shape, you might add an eye, mouth, and the shadow of the nose shape. Think of it as creating a map of the figure with seven continents and adding countries to some of those continents; maybe inside those countries adding states, then within those towns and cities.

Preparation

For this exercise, the following supplies are necessary:

One pad of 18 x 24in (A2) white all-purpose paper or comparable

Charcoal pencils—hard to medium

Kneaded eraser

Directions

Starting from the head again, observe the figure and break it down into seven shapes.

Go into those shapes and start to add other shapes. Perhaps there is an area such as the skirt or top, for example, where a lot of information could be recorded, which you can communicate with a large number of shapes.

To succeed you must use selectivity. If you look at Figure 1 (overleaf), you will see that there is no diversity of shapes or use of selectivity, whereas in Figure 2 you can see selectivity. Look at the figure's right upper torso and arm where there are no additional shapes, or very few, whereas the area immediately adjoining it—the waistline and scarf—are filled with more shapes. The "blank" area is contrasted by a more patterned area, the one framing the other.

Figure 3 is a combination of interesting shapes—contrasting, complementary, large, small. In Figure 4, additional details begin to occupy these shapes, like towns and villages in the various countries of a map, giving depth to the head, defining and contrasting the fabrics of the large evening coat and the intricate bodice, and introducing narrow horizontal details to the waistband and hemline of the skirt to echo and reinforce each other.

Fig. 1

Fig. 2

Fig. 3 Fig. 4

3.4 **Contrasting Shapes**

In this exercise you will be thinking outside the box, or rectangle, or head, or skirt, or arms, or legs, or shadows. Too often it is tempting, when making a drawing composed of shapes, to draw a hair shape, a head shape, a torso shape, an arm shape, a skirt shape, a belt shape, a leg shape, and a shoe shape. Just as you tired of the repetition of the previous sentence, so too will a viewer tire with the obvious in your drawings.

To help counteract this problem, and build on the skills we practiced in the previous sections, we will now concentrate on looking for contrasting shapes. Contrasting shapes are shapes that complement each other in some way—a long shape with a short shape, a vertical with a horizontal, for example. Using contrasting shapes is an important key to holding the attention of the viewer and also in determining your vision. Your selectivity in choosing shapes of different characters that play upon each other not only nurtures your draftsmanship, but also allows you to see anew and reinvent the figure in interesting patterns of varying shapes.

This is similar to the way you used opposition with line. You will again be using all the concepts with which you are now familiar: opposition, verticals, diagonals, horizontals, straight line, curved line, and push and pull. Unconsciously, you were already doing this when you drew the figure in a limited number of shapes. You had to select those most interesting to you and also those that best communicated the figure. Now we are going to apply the idea of contrasting shapes against a backdrop of terms with which you are already acquainted.

Preparation

For this exercise, the following supplies are necessary:

One pad of 18 x 24in (A2) white all-purpose paper or comparable

Charcoal pencils—hard to medium

Kneaded eraser

Opposite: In his portrait of Daniel Craig, John Jay Cabuay employs a series of contrasting shapes: the rounded shape of the actor's face contrasts with the vertical lines of the hand holding the gun; the large shape used to portray the actor's clothes is set against the detail of the face; white is contrasted with black; and the negative shape of the red background is set against the figure.

3.4 Contrasting Shapes

Directions

Throughout this exercise, think about using opposition. You will start by observing the figure and using the premise of five to seven shapes; then begin to communicate the figure in terms of long, short, diagonal, horizontal, busy, simple, and interesting shapes.

Step One

First, analyze the figure in terms of shapes. Are there any shapes visible that are contrasting in character? Look at the figure and try to find shapes of various sizes that are not too repetitive. As in mapping the figure, less is more; if you have only five to seven shapes to choose, select wisely and choose those that will be independent of each other.

In Figure 1, the head and torso combine with the skirt and supporting leg to create a vertical rectangular shape. Played against this elongated shape is the small diagonal face shape and combined arm shape. Glance at the three triangular shapes visible between the negative space of the arms and see how these were pushed slightly to make one narrower and one wider and then played against the horizontal waist shape. All three of these shapes, although close in character, are exaggerated to give each shape a personality. The last shape of the leg uses the slit of the skirt to elongate it and make it more interesting.

Step Two

Expand the horizons of selection by using not only the solid shapes visible, but also the shapes that form shadows, light, folds, or nuances in the pose and clothing that could make for interesting shapes (see Figures 2, 3, 4, 5, and 6).

Figure 2 combines the face and torso shape, while mapping in a smaller busy shape for the shadow of the eyes and the bridge of the nose. The skirt shape is reinvented by using light and shadow on the figure to incorporate the light shape that falls on the rear of the figure and extends the shadow of the skirt shape into the kneecap.

Figure 3 uses the shadow again to reinvent the skirt, while Figures 4, 5, and 6 use the light and texture of the beading on the top to create a specific rounded shape that complements the more angular character of the shadow and folds of the skirt.

Keep in mind that the exercises reflect my personal choices and are indicative of the procedure. There is no right or wrong. Let your inventiveness be a guide and challenge yourself not to be repetitive in selecting the shapes.

Above: In this illustration, Sirichai has used selectivity in his choice of shapes: a single shape encompasses both hands, contrasted with the repetition of the red fingernails, while the solid diagonal shape of the bag contrasts with the more ethereal quality of the hands.

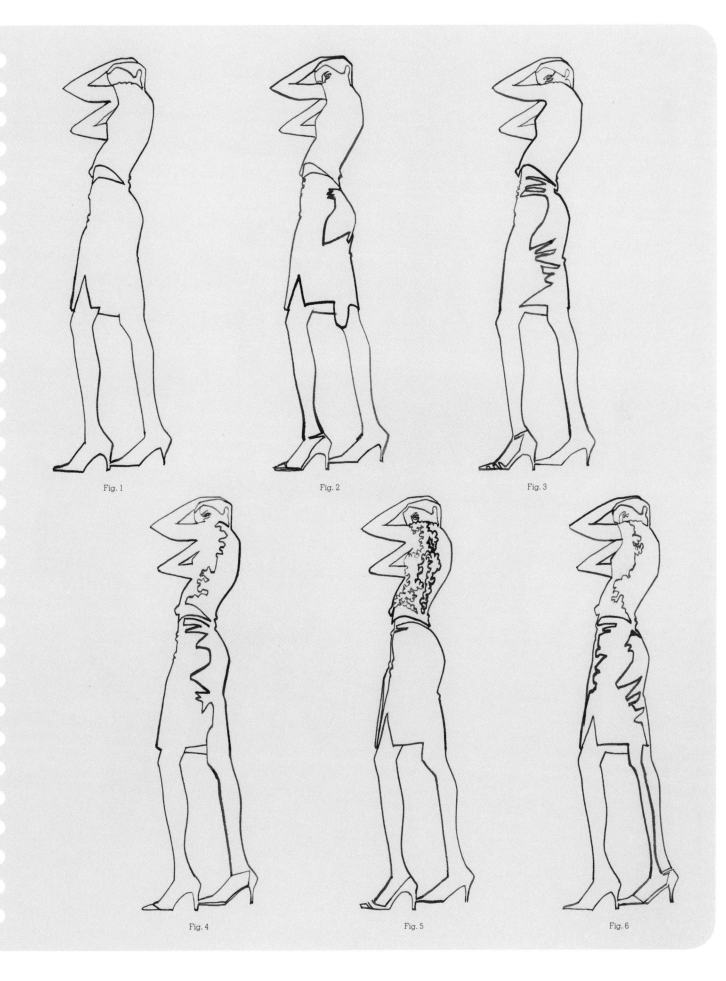

Fig. 1

Fig. 2

Fig. 3

Fig. 4

Fig. 5

Fig. 6

Below: Daniel Egnéus uses one large shape
—the deep mauve of the upholstery—to frame
the figure in this illustration.

3.5 One Large Shape

The bigger the better. Shapes of varying sizes or characteristics create a drawing or illustration that is attractive and will gain the attention of the viewer. That is one of the goals of analyzing the shapes of the figure and choosing accordingly. There are numerous variations on playing and choosing shapes that are different; however, one in particular is a major asset to illustration—locating a large shape within the figure. A large shape can serve as a framing device, a breathing space for the eye, or an area that will complement other shapes of different character. When you allow editing to inform your work, the more minimal and selective your shapes are, and the more important those shapes you do choose become.

In Figure 4 of the Mapping the Figure exercise (see pp. 49–51), the puffa jacket is not only the largest shape, but also the only large shape. It could dominate the drawing, but, played against the other shapes with their different characteristics, it responds to and contrasts with them, rather than monopolizing the figure.

Inside the large shape of the puffa jacket, a continuous line unravels, making indefinite smaller shapes that define its folds and quilting. For the most part, though, the large shape is kept empty and as such gives some breathing space. The use of a large shape not only complements its companion shapes but also adds drama to a drawing. If colored in, it can become a useful backdrop for the visual.

Of course, some poses and clothing naturally lend themselves to a large shape, such as the puffa jacket. However, even in the simplest poses a large shape can be found, either as a discrete area of the body or the clothing, or by combining a few shapes together.

Preparation

For this exercise, the following supplies are necessary:

One pad of 18 x 24in (A2) white all-purpose paper or comparable

Charcoal pencils—hard to medium

Kneaded eraser

3.5 One Large Shape

Step One

Observe the figure. Locate a shape that is large or has the potential of being a large shape. For instance, in Figure 1, in which the model is also wearing a puffy coat, the size of the coat is pushed and exaggerated to make a shape that was large even larger.

Step Two

If the possibility of finding a large shape in the costume or garment of the figure is not viable, then you may combine two or three shapes to make one large shape (see Figure 2).

Step Three

As demonstrated in the Contrasting Shapes exercise (see pp. 53–55), incorporate the shapes inherent in shadows, forms, pleats, light, or characteristics of the clothing. Allow poetic license with a nod toward exaggeration to guide you in selecting and communicating those shapes (see Figure 3).

Step Four

Once you have five to seven shapes, including a large shape, try some mapping within a few shapes to further define the figure (see Figure 4).

Above: This illustration, of John Galliano's Fall 2004 couture collection for Christian Dior, utilizes the large shape of the evening jacket to both frame and complement the silhouette of the figure.

Fig. 1

Fig. 2

Fig. 3

Fig. 4

3.6 Black Shapes

At this point you may be anxious to begin using the vocabulary of different shapes to create a finished drawing. Understandably as artists we like to invest more time in creating a finished drawing than in the preliminaries. Trust in the fact that the time you have invested up to this point was well invested. Every artistic discipline has a foundation formulated to allow the artist to build upon, explore, and nurture their work.

Now that you have attained a knowledge of shapes and line you will be able to use that knowledge consciously or subconsciously to break down a visual quickly and create a drawing that has integrity and is visually graphic, compelling, and solid.

The exercises you have completed so far will serve as a foundation for layering in value, texture, color, or line. In this next exercise we will begin to incorporate solid areas of value, starting with a black shape. Using the same premise as before, we will break the figure up into five to seven simple shapes and then choose one that will best use the black to accentuate the figure.

Preparation

For this exercise, the following supplies are necessary:

One pad of 18 x 24in (A2) white all-purpose paper or comparable

Charcoal pencils—hard to medium

Kneaded eraser

Black pastel or cone

If you have been using a charcoal pencil up to this point, you can color in the black shape with it, but you will be working over a large area and the broad side of a black cone or pastel stick will cover this area more quickly and efficiently.

Opposite: In this illustration for *Residence Magazine*, Bo Lundberg has chosen to portray three areas using one large black shape. This grounds the illustration and defines the table, vase, and TV screen, the figure, and the piano —and also contrasts with the patterned white shape of the chandelier.

3.6 Black Shapes

Directions

The goal of this exercise is to use the black shape to show as much of the figure as possible. We will begin slowly by finding a shape that lends itself to being black. Simple in value, the black will make a stark contrast to the white of the paper and the delicacy of the line. You can also use the black shape to help define one of the positive shapes of the figure by helping to draw what is not visible with five to seven shapes. Therefore, you need to choose your shapes carefully, using the black shape to cover as much of the figure as you can. You can even allow the black shape to break through the boundaries of some of the shapes and encompass more of the figure.

Try to resist the impulse to use the black to color in a small shape like the lips or a pocket or belt buckle for this exercise.

Step One

By now you should be familiar with using selectivity to guide you and with implementing opposition and contrasting shapes. Using these concepts, begin by drawing the figure in five to seven interesting shapes, not including the negative shapes. As in the contrasting and large shape sections (see pp. 52–55 and 56–59), incorporate the shape of shadows or light, or folds and accents specific to the pose and the clothing.

Step Two

Starting at the top of the figure and working your way down, use a black pastel or conté to fill in your chosen shape. In Figure 2, the shape of the hair is filled in before moving down to the collar. You can include some additional mapping of the shapes here to define the features as you progress down through the figure.

Step Three

Following the direction of the shapes, continue to add in the black. Here a diagonal direction is used (see Figure 3).

Step Four

You can choose how to extend the black shape as you continue to work your way down the figure. Here, once the top has been filled in, the decision has been made to continue into the skirt (see Figures 4–5).

Step Five

You can continue to include mapping in the different shapes of the clothing. Here it is used to create more definition in the skirt, where the shape of the shadow on the skirt is penciled in to guide the movement of the black (see Figure 6).

Step Six

Continue to extend the black shape down through the figure. Here the black shape has been extended to the hem of the skirt before breaking through the hemline of the right leg and defining the shape of the shadow on the leg (see Figures 7–8).

Step Seven

The black shape can be used to add definition. In Figures 9–11 the black is used to add definition to the supporting leg and shoe.

Step Eight

Finally, black can be used to add detail to the figure. Here it is used to fill in smaller shapes like the upper lip and fingernails (see Figure 12).

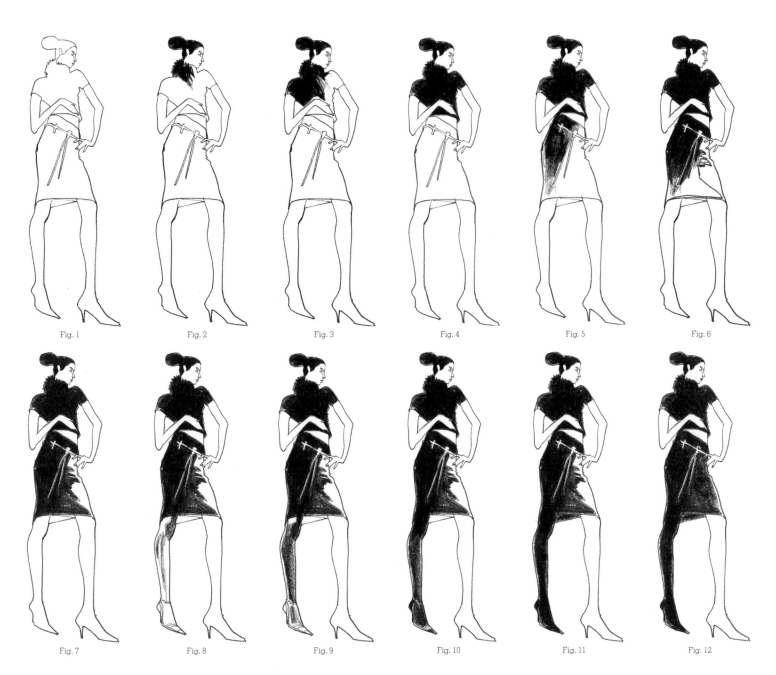

Fig. 1   Fig. 2   Fig. 3   Fig. 4   Fig. 5   Fig. 6

Fig. 7   Fig. 8   Fig. 9   Fig. 10   Fig. 11   Fig. 12

3.7 Gray Shapes

Not everything in life is in black or white. Black with white makes for a powerful graphic, but one that could have limitations. Black and white lack value, the ingredient that can provide a greater sense of depth.

In this exercise, we will use gray to accent and complement the black and white areas of a drawing, adding depth and form to the figure. This exercise will also help you to see the figure in terms of gray. The addition of a gray area or shape allows the illustration to reflect the nuances visible in the figure such as the shadows or highlights as well as the tints and tones of the features and skin. Black was used in the last exercise to aid selectivity and help communicate as much of the figure as possible. Its use was limited to areas within the clothing or to depict shadows; it was not used to describe the skin, face, or features other than the lips. The addition of a gray shape creates variety and interest and can be used as a tool to describe the darks and lights on a figure. Gray can best be used to communicate those areas that black would distort or abstract.

There are numerous methods for exploring the grays in the figure and, combined with different media, there are endless variations. Here we will be completing two exercises that accomplish this goal.

Preparation

For this exercise, the following supplies are necessary:

One pad of 18 x 24in (A2) white all-purpose paper or comparable

Three gray conté crayons or similar pastels, preferably in the cool rather than the warm family:

1. Light gray

2. Medium gray

3. Dark gray

Depending on the size of your drawing, using pastels for this technique can be awkward. It may be difficult to capture a small area of a shape using a large unsharpened tool. Using a thin pastel stick or conté rather than a large pastel will allow you to define the area more successfully. Although a colored pencil might be ideal to cover the smaller areas, it has its limitations in expressing weight and depth and it is too time-consuming to use for covering a large area of the figure. If you are using a model, have the model do a series of three to five ten-minute poses.

Opposite: In his illustration, *All Cats are Gray*, John Jay Cabuay uses gray shapes to depict the hat and lips in contrast to the white of the skin tone and the black used for the hair and eye shapes. The use of gray softens the harshness of the black and results in a very graphic image in which the eyes are the most arresting feature.

Fig. 1

Fig. 2

Fig. 3

Fig. 4

Fig. 5

Fig. 6

3.7 Exercise 1: Gray Shapes with Line

Directions

For this exercise you will be asked to communicate the figure in four values: white, light gray, medium gray, and dark gray. Analyze the figure in terms of a gray scale, from light to dark. The lightest will be represented by white (in other words, do not fill in this area); darkest will be represented by the dark gray medium. Between these two ends of the scale you will use the light and middle gray media.

Step One

Before you put conté or pastel to paper, visually break the figure up into five to seven simple, interesting shapes. Using the lightest gray, draw the figure with line in those five to seven shapes. Use your selectivity and incorporate nuances or shadows that you feel would describe the figure (see Figure 1).

Step Two

Once you have drawn the figure, begin at the top and start laying in your lightest grays; if an area is the lightest, select that area as a white shape to play against the grays. Attempt to fill in the shape completely to the edge of the line so that the line is almost obscured. Continue through the figure until you have colored in all of the light gray shapes you selected (see Figure 2).

Step Three

Next, begin adding in the middle grays, again starting at the top of the figure and working your way down (see Figure 3).

Step Four

Complete the layering of values with the darkest value (see Figure 4).

Step Five

Once completed, if necessary, map in some additional shapes to realize the figure fully (see Figures 5–6).

If you have completed this task and want to challenge your eye and skill a bit further, continue to Exercise 2 (overleaf).

Note:
Find several high-contrast photos of darks and lights from a newspaper or magazine. Draw a frame and use the premise of the gray shapes to organize the darks and lights from the photo into the frame. See the darks and lights as shapes. Attempt the same exercise using a color such as sepia or brown. After several attempts using the sepia colors, try the same exercise using one color in a monochromatic scheme. Add black and white to vary the values of the color.

68

Fig. 1

Fig. 2

Fig. 3

Fig. 4

Fig. 5

Fig. 6

Fig. 7

Fig. 8

Fig. 9

Fig. 10

Fig. 11

3.7 Exercise 2: Gray Shapes without Line

Directions

In this exercise we will avoid using line to draw in the gray shapes initially, and instead will draw the gray shape area without an outline.

Step One

Starting again at the top of the figure, begin to draw in the shape of the first value you see—in this instance, the hair shape. Color that shape in fully before proceeding to the next shape (see Figure 1).

Step Two

Move slowly through the figure, filling in each shape. Continue in a rhythmic motion until you have completed the figure (see Figures 2–10).

The absence of line is a good method to train your eye and will sharpen your draftsmanship. It is easier to fill in the simple larger areas than the more intricate areas such as the hands. If you feel the need to draw in the shape of the smaller areas and then fill them in, give yourself permission to do so. It is a greater challenge, however, to complete and color each shape as you progress.

As in Exercise 1 (see pp. 66–67), leave those areas that are lightest white and use the gray to hold those areas of clothing. Here the light gray is used to hold the scarf shape.

Step Three

The absence of line may mean that some areas of the figure are not defined. Incorporating some elements of the environment, such as the model platform, wall, or shapes visible in the pose, may help to define such areas (see Figure 11).

Note:
Choose two complementary colors such as red and green. Create a landscape within a frame, preferably from observation. It could be a view from a window, a park, or taken from a photo. Analyze the visual and recreate it in light, medium, and dark values. Use the complementary colors (red and green, or purple and yellow, for example) to create the three values. Layer one color onto another to create a mixed neutral color. Increase the saturation of one color to vary the darks and lights within the image.

Stina Persson's haunting image uses negative
shapes, framing the face and leaf shapes with
light washes of watercolor.

3.8 Negative Shapes

Accentuate the negative. Your visual vocabulary should now include a solid understanding of shapes. You may even be seeing life in a different way and breaking up everything in terms of shapes. This is not unusual; I have had many students comment that everywhere they turn they see shapes. It is the same as learning a new language; when you are finally able to communicate in that language, everything begins to make sense.

Selectivity has been the guiding premise throughout this book. Your knowledge of editing and your ability to communicate the figure with fewer lines or shapes will now come into play with an exercise that will use absence of value or line to draw an area of the figure.

What you leave out will be just as important as what you choose to convey. In any drawing, the viewer recognizes those areas left out, usually by their shape. To make these shapes, which are known as negative shapes, recognizable, you need to use the adjoining shapes to bookend and frame the negative space. To achieve this, you may have to create a pose with the model whereby some of the figure that will be communicated as the negative shape is backdropped by shapes of solid value; for example, an arm held across the figure, where the arm is the negative shape, is framed by the darker value of the clothing.

Incorporating a large shape and perhaps one in black will best accentuate the negative shape. If the pose of the figure does not accomplish this then incorporate some of the environment or add a graphic element or shape to backdrop the area that is in a negative form. In the previous Gray Shapes without Line exercise, for example, the platform was incorporated into Figure 11 to help describe the negative area of the pant leg. You could also add a line here and there to help define some of the negative area.

Preparation

For this exercise, the following supplies are necessary:

One pad of 18 x 24in (A2) white all-purpose paper or comparable

At this point you can bring in different media, such as ink. The use of digital techniques also makes its first appearance in this exercise, with the use of Photoshop. Color is also added for the first time.

3.8 Negative Shapes

Directions

Observe the pose of the figure and think how best to use the positive shapes to frame the negative shapes. Could you use a large shape, perhaps a black one that might hold the whole figure? Areas that are light in value are easiest to use as the negative shapes. Positioning these areas in front of the solid shapes, such as placing the arms in front of a black area, will create a backdrop to hold the negative shapes.

Begin at the top of the figure and start drawing in a shape and filling it in before you progress to the next area.

Fill in the shape as in the Gray Shapes exercises. When you arrive at the shape that is negative, use your draftsmanship skills to put in the next shape without drawing a line to hold it. Be courageous! Your failures will determine your growth far more than your successes. Be willing to make mistakes and do not pencil in the area as a guide to fill in later. That would be counter-productive to training your eye. In the future it may be prudent to do this, but for now use whatever skills you have and make the leap.

Step One

First decide which is your negative shape. In this exercise, the decision was made to have the lightest area, the skin, as the negative shape. The shape of the hair, therefore, was filled in to hold the face shape. The eye rather than the brush was used to mentally draw the figure from the edge of the ears to the neck in order to place in the neckline and shoulders of the dress (see Figure 1).

Step Two

You can add the shape of the features to help define the face (see Figure 2).

Step Three

Continue to carefully draw around the negative shapes. Here, the arms are defined as the negative shape. The beading on the dress is also used as a series of negative shapes (see Figure 3).

Step Four

Use a solid value to fill in the areas around the negative shapes. In Figure 4 solid black is used to help bookmark the negative shape of the arms. The beading was revisited and edited a bit more.

Step Five

Try to find shapes that complement each other. The legs were drawn initially as one gray shape in Figure 5 to see how this would complement the black shape. The stool acts as a linear contour shape in light gray, and opposition is used to give character to the negative spaces between its legs. The splash of ink, although not intentional, was kept as a choice.

Step Six

Continue to refine your drawing, looking at how the shapes work with each other. Here, the leg shape, which had been filled in as one gray value, looked visually confusing. To correct this mistake and separate the legs, a deeper gray was used to fill in the back leg shape and accentuate the front leg left in a lighter gray (see Figure 6).

Step Seven

Notice that in Figure 6 your eye will fill in the shape of the back arm as well as the shape of the neck and head so that the drawing is complete. Figure 7 shows how to further define the negative shapes by drawing in the shape of the neck and the back arm in pencil and using Photoshop to add a rectangular frame of color.

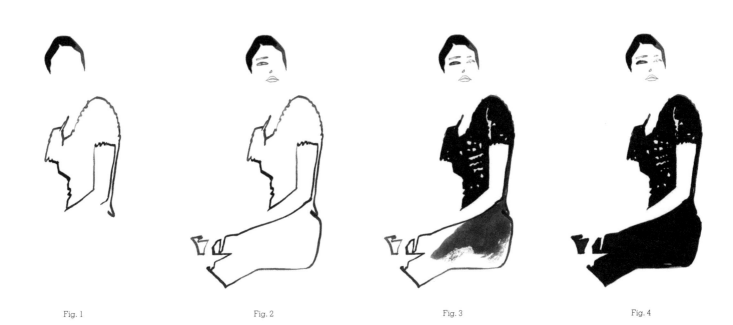

Fig. 1   Fig. 2   Fig. 3   Fig. 4

Fig. 5   Fig. 6   Fig. 7

Below: In this series of unpublished sketches by Antonio Lopez, entitled *Amelia*, for Bloomingdales department store, we can see how the preliminary studies of line and value developed into a finished illustration of dark and light shapes.

3.9 Dark and Light Values

In simple terms, value means the darkness or lightness of a color. A light source will illuminate the figure and play upon its various planes and contours, casting a shadow in those areas not directly visible to the light. Light and shadow are elements that not only create depth but also allow for an observation of the form and a particular rendering of the form.

In photography, shapes of light and shadow are incorporated into the composition, and the photographer has a trained eye to decipher these shapes. The same principles apply to drawing. The following exercises allow you to deconstruct the figure in terms of lights and darks, and show you how to recognize and select those shapes. Now that you have a good command of shapes, it should be easier to break down the figure in these terms.

There are numerous methods to explore the values on the figure. In the following three exercises we will use the light, medium, and dark values to communicate the lights and darks. In the Gray Shape exercises, we began to explore the idea of incorporating the values of the figure into the drawing, whether it was a shadow on the face or the clothing. Now we will focus on capturing and exaggerating the light areas and the shadows that form on the figure due to a strong sense of light.

In the first exercise the goal is to communicate the figure entirely through the presence of the shadow that is cast by a strong light source. In the second you will focus on the light areas and, for the first time, we will begin to consider composition by introducing a frame. In the third we will combine the use of light and dark values from the previous two exercises, creating a truly three-dimensional figure.

Preparation

For these exercises the following supplies are necessary:

For the first exercise, colored paper of a light value, such as a pale gray, taupe, or brown.

For the second exercise, colored paper that is dark enough in value to show off the white, black, and gray conté charcoal, pastel, or pencil. If the idea of using a color seems attractive, choose one that will not wrestle with the white for attention. Avoid colors that are neon or too bright as they will compromise and overwhelm the drawing of the light on the figure.

For the third exercise, use a colored paper that will be medium in value to allow the addition of a dark and light medium.
You will also need:
Black charcoal or pastel
White conté, pastel, or pencil
Gray conté, pastel, or pencil

You will need to have a strong light source to exaggerate the lights and shadows of the figure. Position the light source to the left or right of the model to create this play of darks and lights on the figure.

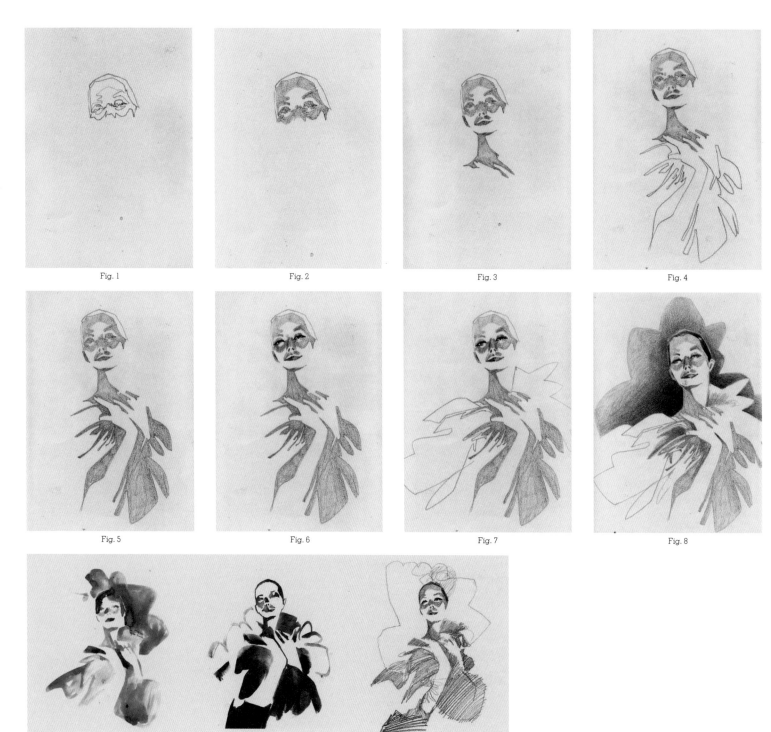

Fig. 1

Fig. 2

Fig. 3

Fig. 4

Fig. 5

Fig. 6

Fig. 7

Fig. 8

Fig. 9

3.9 Exercise 1: Dark Values

Directions

In this exercise, you will be working with a limited palette of black and various tones of black that form grays. You will be using those values to communicate solely the shapes of the shadow on the figure without using any outside line to define the figure. The figure will be defined only by the shapes of shadows. The light areas of the figure will be seen as negative shapes and will be the color of the paper. Depending on the direction of light, there may be a shadow of the figure in the background that could be incorporated into the drawing to accentuate, contrast, and hold the white areas of the figure.

Step One

Observe the form of the figure, particularly the shapes of the shadow on the figure from the top down. It may be prudent to do a series of quick studies to see how you might select and interpret the shadows (see Figure 9). To better discern the shapes of the shadows, you can squint; this will eliminate the shadows that are not prominent. Be decisive; if there is an area you are unsure about, leave it out—just communicate the areas that are most visible. Use a very light line to first draw in the shape of the shadow. When you have completed an area, begin to fill in that shape with a light to medium gray value (see Figures 1–2). If you are using a charcoal pencil, lightly color in the shape to the same value as the outside line, much as we did in the Gray Shape with Line exercise (see pp. 66–67).

Step Two

Continue drawing in the shadow shapes, gradually filling in each section as you progress through the figure. Emphasis should be placed on the face (see Figures 3–5) .

Step Three

Once you have drawn and filled in all of the shadow shapes selected, observe the figure once again. Starting at the top of the figure, begin to fine-tune the features and layer in the darker-value shapes to further define the figure.

Notice that by using the shape of the shadow without a definitive outside line you have drawn the figure as well as most of the definition of the figure. At this point in the drawing, your selection will become more important; your editing decisions will affect the graphics of the visual. Remember that less is more (see Figures 6–7).

Step Four

Usually when you are using a strong light source there will be an interesting shadow that may help define the areas not drawn. A shadow is the perfect device for poetic license and allows the artist to stylize and use the shadow as a graphic component. In Figure 8, the background shadow is stylized into the shape of a flower, which mimicks the model's garment and complements and frames the negative shapes. Alternatively, you could use a geometrical element that may be a feature of the background to serve as a framing device.

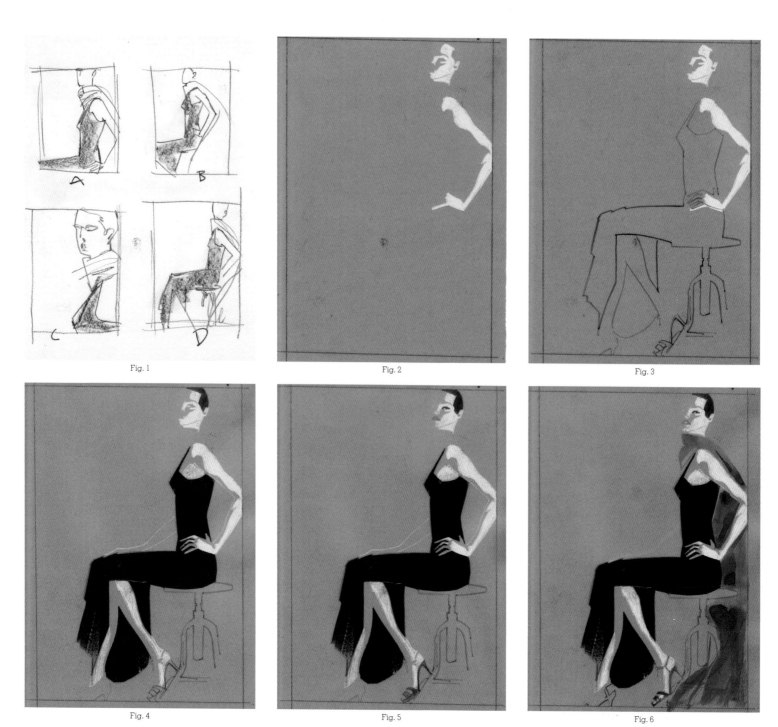

Fig. 1

Fig. 2

Fig. 3

Fig. 4

Fig. 5

Fig. 6

3.9 Exercise 2: Light Values

Directions

You probably noticed in the previous exercise that while you were drawing in the dark shadows of the figure you were also capturing the light areas. In this exercise, the focus will be on those light areas; you will also be incorporating a large shape to help anchor the light shapes. Light does not have boundaries when directed at the model; it envelops the whole figure. For this exercise, however, we will limit the light to just the face and skin and use a large black shape to anchor and contrast the white shapes. This exercise will also introduce the idea of drawing a frame on your paper in which to place the figure. Previously, we have been focusing on the idea of composing the figure with shapes; drawing a frame will also allow you to think about the shape of the entire figure and how best to compose that shape within a given space.

Step One

Draw a small frame onto your paper. You can draw this by hand or with a ruler depending on your personal taste. Observe the figure and think about composition, or how you would like to position the figure within the frame. Seeing the figure as a shape should give you an advantage in placing this shape within the frame. Think about the space not being occupied by the figure. The space that is not occupied is as important as the space occupied.

Into this frame do a simple contour drawing of the figure in a light pencil, not unlike the ones we drew in Chapter 1. Simplify the figure and keep the shape clean and empty. Place the figure wherever you think best shows it off within the frame. You may wish to move it to the left or right or, more dramatically, crop the figure. If cropping the figure is your choice, make sure to crop the figure in a manner where the face or part of the face is visible (see Figure 1).

Step Two

Observe the figure, this time focusing on the white or light cast upon it. Draw in the shape of the light areas from the top down with your white medium and then carefully fill in the selected shapes until the figure or your selection is complete. Unlike the previous exercise there will be no layering in of the brightest value on the figure. A subtlety in the shading and use of the white may capture the nuances in the light, but a solid white would work just as well (see Figure 2).

Step Three

If the necessity of drawing in some of the figure allows you to place some of the light on the figure accurately, then draw that area in a light line that you can eventually fill in (see Figure 3).

Step Four

Once the white is complete, analyze the figure to see if there are any solid areas that may complement the white areas, such as the hair or clothing, or a large shape that will help communicate the areas that are not visible (see Figure 4).

Step Five

Once the figure is defined, begin to fine-tune the details or features if necessary. Fine-tuning your drawing should occur toward the end rather than in the beginning. This way you will leave yourself open to the options of what and what not to edit. Here the face is defined with the addition of an eye, while a little color has been brought into the picture by using red to define the lips (see Figure 5).

Step Six

Finally, the back arm was deleted and, instead of using a shadow behind the figure, the scarf was used to define the negative shape. The scarf was added in a gray value so as not to distract from the black and also to hold the negative shape between the arm and body and define the edge of the frame (see Figure 6).

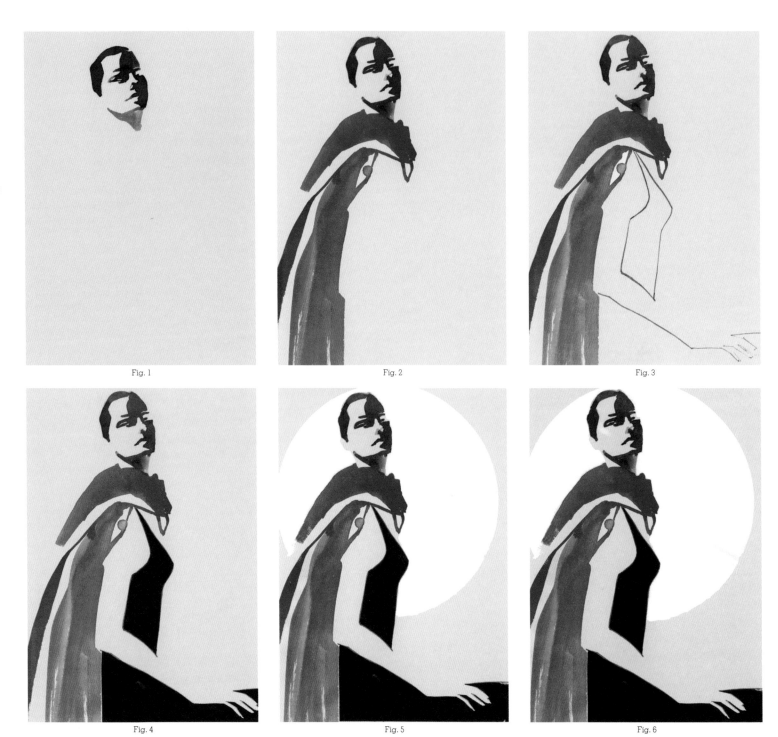

Fig. 1   Fig. 2   Fig. 3

Fig. 4   Fig. 5   Fig. 6

3.9 Exercise 3: Dark and Light Values Combined

Directions

To continue this journey of communicating values, we will now combine the two previous exercises into one drawing. When lighting the figure you have probably already discovered that the values are nuanced in tone. For the purposes of simplifying the figure it is best to limit these many tonalities and retain a graphic dynamic. You can do this by limiting the palette in the same way you did in the gray exercises where light, medium, and dark grays were used (see pp. 66–69).

Again, be selective. Since the dark value will simultaneously define the light value and vice versa, select whichever seems the more prominent and use the alternate value sparingly as a simple accent. You can also incorporate black as well as a negative shape and try out color or use a different medium.

Be courageous and explore the various options. As artists we learn much more through failure than success, and unless you are willing to fail you will never achieve the latter. An accident may be the genesis of a new direction and be responsible for a fantastic image.

Step One

After doing a few studies, tackle the figure directly from the top of the composition. Decide which value—dark or light—will dictate the figure and apply accordingly (see Figure 1).

Step Two

You can use the garment to create a graphic element; in Figure 2 the red scarf has been used.

Step Three

Analyze the drawing. Think about where and what to incorporate next; is there an area that could be identified as a negative shape? If there is, define it with line and fill in with the same value (see Figures 3–4).

Step Four

At this point, decide on a graphic element to include in the background to complement the figure. Use your imagination (see Figure 5).

Step Five

Once completed, add in the alternate value to define and accent the figure; in this case a subtle definition of light on cheekbone and eyelid has been used (see Figure 6).

Chapter Four
Line Quality

Line is the pulse of a drawing. It can beat like a drum or rise
and fall like the notes of a violinist. It is limitless in its possibilities
and nuances. It can be sensual, reserved, immediate, studious,
or minimal; it can wreak havoc or organize chaos; it can capture
emotion, energy, movement, and flair all at once.

Line has no boundaries; it is as limitless as the artist's imagination.
Line is an extension of the artist's personality. It emulates from a
physical connection of hand, medium, and surface. Egon Schiele
defined his drawings with a selective, sensual line of varying weight;
Tina Berning's fluidity of line has a life of its own; while John Jay
Cabuay's confidence and command of line surfaces as a rhythmic
form of energy.

Until this point we have been using contour line as a tool. A
contour line is a descriptive device to form designated shapes.
The contour line we utilized had no personality. It was of one value
without any nuances of color, movement, or weight. The grace and
versatility of line, absent in the previous chapters, will now come into
play. Shapes will be ever-present and important as we proceed
through this chapter; your knowledge of shapes will allow you to
utilize line confidently and nurture your draftsmanship and eye.

In this chapter we explore line quality—the character and variety
of line as demonstrated through the use of weight, texture, or value.
Line quality can be evasive, as it is derived from an individual
perspective and will have a personal relationship to its creator.
There are some guidelines, however, to help nurture an understanding
of line quality and allow those ideas to filter through the drawing
in a cohesive manner that will flow through the figure. The following
foreground, middle-ground, and background exercises are devised
to simplify line quality in terms of dark, medium, and light values
that will be used to communicate depth and space.

Composition, which has been touched upon in previous exercises,
will rise to the fore and will play an intricate role in communicating
those same ideas of depth and space.

4.1 Foreground, Middle Ground, and Background

Preparation

For the next three exercises, the following supplies are necessary:

One pad of 18 x 24in (A2) white all-purpose paper or comparable

Charcoal pencils—hard to medium

Kneaded eraser

The use of a model as well as three separate model stands is ideal for this exercise. "Ideal" is the key word; I have often taught classes where only one model stand was available and I moved that model stand accordingly to reflect the three different positions we will use in these exercises. When no model stand was available, masking tape was applied to the floor space to form similar square areas.

The idea of introducing line works best when using a live model. If, however, a photo is the only option available, choose three different photos of fashion figures that are the same size in scale and are viewed from the same eye level or perspective; you can substitute the three photos for the three positions of the model.

Position the first of the model stands closest to your drawing area, which will be the foreground figure. Next, position the second model stand farther away for the middle-ground figure, and position a third stand as far away as possible for, of course, the background figure.

Above: Melanie Reim's image, *Racetrack*, uses different qualities of line in the foreground, middle, and background. A continuous line of energy flows in a diagonal movement back and forth across the composition, boldly defining figures in the foreground, suggesting activity in the middle ground, while blurring the imagery in the background. Reim's skilled eye and deft hand coordinate in a seemingly effortless quick motion to give depth to the composition and interest to the characters, drawing the viewer into the image.

4.1 Exercise 1: Foreground

Directions

Have the model assume a pose on the first model stand (the foreground position).

Onto your paper draw a square framed area, 10 x 10in (25 x 25cm) or larger. Observe the figure and think about how you will position this figure within the framed space. You will need to pay attention to the composition of the various figures in your drawing and how they are positioned in the given space. It is perfectly permissible, and indeed preferable, to overlap and eventually crop the figures.

This first drawing will be considered as a drawing of the figure in the foreground. This is the figure that is closest to the viewer and therefore will be the largest figure or shape in the frame. This figure could be exaggerated; the space this figure occupies should be given great attention. Cropping of this figure is necessary to create exaggeration.

All foreground figures will most likely monopolize a great deal of the positive space but leaving room for the addition of other figures.

Step One

The foreground figure is cropped and positioned to the right with areas of negative space (see Figure 1). Begin to draw the model within your frame with a solid black and exaggerated thick contour line. Continue to see in terms of shape, although in this exercise you do not need to be so strict about only drawing shapes.

Step Two

Draw the foreground figure in a framed space as before, but with a tighter crop (see Figure 2). This "close-up shot" should be positioned to the right and divide the compositional space in half.

Step Three

The foreground figure should now be centered in the framed space (see Figure 3), leaving negative spaces for the inclusion of additional figures.

Above: In this composition, I made the foreground figure occupy the full height of the frame, placing the image to the left and cropping it to create exaggeration.

Fig. 1

Fig. 2

Fig. 3

4.1 Exercise 2: Middle Ground

Directions

Next, have the model take a pose on the middle-ground model stand. Observe and think about the placement of this figure. Keep in mind that you will need to leave enough space for a background figure to be incorporated into the space as well. When drawing the middle-ground figure, use a thinner gray line in contrast to the value of the line used for the foreground figure. Be creative with your placement of this figure; crop again if need be and think how the model's position might best serve the composition of the foreground figure.

Step One

Take the first composition for the previous exercise (see pp. 84–85) and add in a middle-ground figure. Make it smaller in scale, lighter in tone, and positioned to left of the original foreground figure, as if exiting the framed space (see Figure 1). Draw the middle-ground figure's head turned toward the viewer, bringing the attention back to the foreground figure.

Step Two

Now take the second compostion from the previous exercise. Include a middle-ground figure, positioned directly behind and overlapping with the foreground figure (see Figure 2), thus creating a greater sense of depth.

Step Three

Using the final composition from the previous exercise, add in a middle-ground figure that is much smaller in scale (see Figure 3). This will create an exaggerated sense of space.

Above: The shoes placed in the middle ground in the compositions by Gabriel Ayala (top), Tim Patterson (bottom left), and Cesar de la Rosa (bottom right) are drawn with a finer, gray line and are overlapped by the foreground shoes to create a sense of space.

Fig. 1

Fig. 2

Fig. 3

4.1 Exercise 3: Background

Directions

Now have the model take a pose on the third model stand and use this for the background figure. Look at your compositon of the foreground and middle-ground figures. Think about where best to place the background figure within the space.

The line to communicate the background figure should be faint and airy, almost on the verge of disappearing. This line should have no resemblance to the lines of the other occupants of the space. Using this faint line, draw the entire figure. Place this figure far in the background to create a contrast with the large cropped foreground figure. If the foreground figure is the largest then the background figure will be the smallest, probably drawn from head to toe, and will disappear into the background. If it suits the composition, the figure can be cropped to the left or right, or drawn behind one of the foreground figures or another in the background.

Observe the composition of the three figures and evaluate whether you are satisfied with the arrangement. Is there space for additional figures farther in the background? Would these figures enhance or detract from the current composition?

Once you understand the idea of drawing the figure with different line qualities, the use of three model platforms is unneccesary. One model stand in the same position will suffice. Have the model take a pose and decide whether to use the pose for your foreground, middle, or background figure. It is easier to begin this exercise with the placement of the foreground figure, as that is usually the figure that takes up most space; however, it is up to your personal sense of composition as to how to begin the placement of figures. I would advise, nevertheless, always saving the background figures for the final placement.

Step One

Following the first composition from the previous exercise (pp. 86–87), add in a background figure that is is smaller in scale and lighter in tone than the middle-ground figure (see Figure 1). Position this behind the foreground figure, creating depth. Additional background figures (also lighter in tone) break up the compositional space and create the illusion of further space.

Step Two

Taking the second composition from the previous exercise, draw a background figure that is cropped out of the framed space, but facing into it (see Figure 2). This brings the focus on to the foreground figure.

Step Three

For the third composition, the middle-ground figure from the final composition in the previous exercise (see p. 87) is turned into a background figure. This is achieved by the addition of a new figure that is larger in scale and deeper in value (see Figure 3). Again, additional background figures divide the space and create depth.

Above: *Meow Mix* is a preliminary inked drawing that demonstrates how line quality and scale can be used to communicate depth and space. Color was later incorporated into the illustration via Photoshop.

Fig. 1

Fig. 2

Fig. 3

90

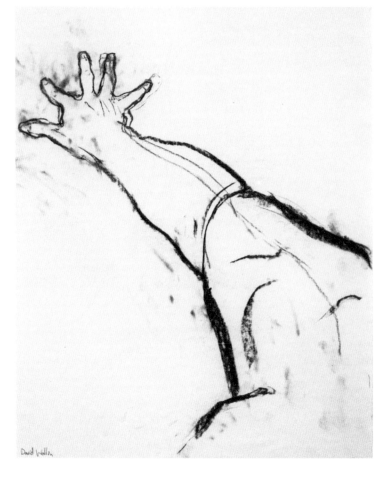

4.2 **Using Line Quality to Illustrate Depth on the Figure**

If you accomplished the goal of creating depth in a given space by using three lines of different weights and values, then you will easily be able to translate that premise into this exercise. The previous exercise used line variation to communicate space and depth by using a thick, dark line to represent the figure in the foreground and a faint thin line to represent the figure in the background. The middle-ground figure was of a line quality somewhere in between that of the foreground and that of the background.

Those three line qualities will now be used to translate depth onto a single figure. The premise is the same. The area of the figure closest to you would be considered the foreground area and, therefore, will be drawn with the darkest, thickest line, and so on. There are two minor differences between these two exercises: the flow and the merge.

The flow of the line and how seamlessly it merges into different line qualities will depend on how much pressure you exert on the charcoal, pencil, or brush you use.

Preparation

For the next three exercises, the following supplies are necessary:

One pad of 18 x 24in (A2) white all-purpose paper or comparable

Charcoal pencils—hard to medium

Kneaded eraser

To help distinguish the features on the model that are closest to you from those farther away, ask the model to take a pose that exaggerates this idea, for example, thrusting one arm forward and positioning the other one behind her.

Note:
This is a practical skill that will take a little practice. You can always use a scrap piece of paper, and, starting from the top of the page, slowly draw a very pale line that gradates into a thick, dark line as it reaches the bottom of the page. Create variations on this exercise as you feel more confident, going from thick to thin to thick, and so on.

Opposite: Line quality alone can give movement, weight, and depth to any drawing, as evidenced by this selection of work by Eva Hjelte (top left), Barbara Pearlman (top right), Joe Eula (below left), and David Wallin (below right).

4.2 Using Line Quality to Illustrate Depth on the Figure

Directions

In this exercise we will incorporate all three line qualities into one line to draw one figure. The idea remains the same, but this line will have a bit more energy and variance as it evolves from a thin pale line to a thick dark line and vice versa.

Step One

Proceed slowly to start with. Think in terms of shapes when observing, and make an allowance for the flow of your line to move freely around the figure.

Press slightly down onto the paper with your medium and start with the middle ground, or center of the figure, using the quality of line here to inform the foreground and the background lines (see Figures 1–2).

Step Two

Push the difference of weights between the thick and thin lines as they describe the figure. Skim the surface with your charcoal as you draw the areas farthest away lighter and smaller. Exaggerate what is closer by making it a little larger in scale and by pressing harder to give a darker, thicker line (see Figures 3–5).

The method you improvise will depend on your view of the figure and confidence in handling the medium. Keep in mind the ideas incorporated in Chapter 2, which addressed verticals, diagonals, and horizontals in the figure, and use this information as an additional guide to move your line through the figure. Using line quality is an intuitive process and this exercise is a guide to nurture your exploration of line quality. The drawing need not be tight. It would be a disservice to nurture a line rich in line quality and have it be contained and strained. Give it freedom of mobility.

Fig. 1   Fig. 2

Fig. 3   Fig. 4   Fig. 5

4.3 Continuous Line

Con-tin-u-ous adjective
1. continuing without changing, stopping, or being interrupted in space or time.
Encarta World English Dictionary

If we now merge the definition of continuous with that of line quality and think rhythm, music, energy, grace, flow, and sensuality, we have a definition of continuous line.

As you may have noticed in the previous exercise, the textured cables of the sweater and the folds of the skirt of the middle area of the figure were handled in a continuous line method. The line was allowed to glide over the area and was not too exact in replicating what was present.

A continuous line has a life of its own and should be allowed the freedom to explore the white space of paper as a continuum of the artist's vision. Imagine a violinist playing a piece of music. As the violinist plays, note the consistent gliding of the bow back and forth across the strings, in turn creating an unbroken musical line that rises and falls in volume, tempo, and artistic interpretation. All arts are related on many levels and one of the universal themes in art is how the artist, author, or musician allows a personal vision to intuitively affect and influence their work.

Continuous line is an ideal place to consider how to incorporate an individualistic viewpoint into your work. A line that flows through the hand to the paper as a result of observation is relative to the artist's relationship to the visual. This cannot be taught. It is a learned skill developed through practice, integrity, and a passion for drawing. It is an experience unique to the individual, and what is right for one artist may be the antithesis of the ideal for another.

What can be taught, however, is a method to begin to explore these ideas. Therefore, in this exercise, we will look at some ideas of continuous line.

Preparation

For this exercise, the following supplies are necessary:

One pad of 18 x 24in (A2) white all-purpose paper or comparable

Charcoal, pencil, pastel, crayons, markers, pen, oil stick, or any medium that can move without needing to be replenished

Note:
There is only one rule for this exercise: once you put pencil or charcoal to paper you will make a commitment to complete the drawing without lifting your medium off the paper. That's it.

Opposite: The flamboyant qualities and movement of the cancan dancers' costumes are perfectly portrayed by Rachel Ann Lindsay using continuous line, in which the pen never leaves the page.

Directions

The goal with continuous line is to allow a freedom of movement and enable a trust between your eye and hand. The line should sweep and glide and examine areas with no regard to borders or boundaries. This freedom to move every which way could court chaos and not make sense visually. Therefore, a keen sense of selectivity and observation will nurture a more studied and descriptive drawing.

Where your drawing commences will be up to you. This is an opportunity to recreate your drawings in a different way, so you might want to start your drawing in a place you have never started from before; maybe the middle of the figure, the eye, or the feet.

Here are some initial guidelines to help you begin investigating continuous lines.

Step One

Choose an area near the top of the figure as a starting point and have your line move diagonally through the figure to an ascertained ending point. Have your line slowly move back and forth between these two points (see Figure 1).

Step Two

Use the idea of shapes, negative, large, or otherwise, to border the continuous line and control chaos (see Figure 2).

Step Three

Layer in the line to create a deeper value, as you did in the Dark Values exercise (see pp. 76–77). It is acceptable to backtrack and layer in a deeper value to help describe some areas.

To give additional depth and interest to the drawing, incorporate some of the line quality used in the previous exercise (see pp. 92–93). Use pressure and, thinking about the violinist, vary the pressure on your medium to create a variety of line quality (see Figure 3).

Step Four

When the drawing is almost complete, evaluate which areas of the drawing might need some additional information to clarify the visual. Add a second color or begin to add a second continuous line that emanates from a different area than the first line (see Figure 4).

Explore different variations of continuous line as well as exploring different media or combinations. A stiff line that zig-zags through the drawing has a harder edge and could be ideal to capture a male figure; a more studied, angular line can be incorporated to describe architectural features (see p. 98, Figures 5–8); a fluid, soft line that swirls can be used to denote softness or textured patterns such as lace, embroidery, or hair (see p. 99, Figures 9–12).

The key to using a continuous line is to allow the line the freedom to move through the figure with light-handed guidance from the artist. It is playful in nature, so use this playfulness to your advantage. Don't restrict its movement or your possibilities.

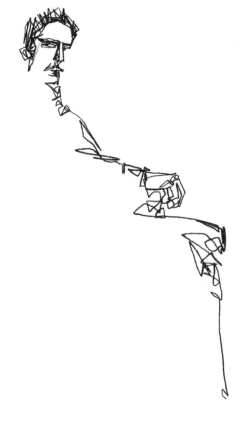

Fig. 1

Fig. 2

Fig. 3

Fig. 4

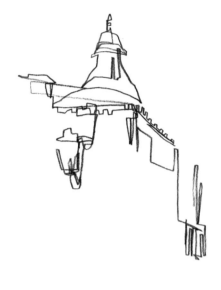

Fig. 5

Fig. 6

Fig. 7

Fig. 8

Fig. 9

Fig. 10

Fig. 11

Fig. 12

4.4 Studious Line

The studious line and the continuous line both share the characteristic of a traveling line. However, while the continuous line travels across the figure in a somewhat rhythmic flow, the studious line is observant, slowly capturing a particular area within the figure.

The aim of the studious line is to capture as much information as possible with fine attention to detail as it moves from one location to another. Unlike the continuous line, the flow of a studious line can be broken if it seems necessary to invest time in another area of interest; so, while the line may flow in a specific direction it can also linger on an area until it has been duly captured before moving on. A studious line is adept at capturing patterns, prints, and features such as the eyes, recording every eyelash, or the intricacy of flowing hair. While being very observant, the studious line is also a free spirit.

Preparation

For this exercise, the following supplies are necessary:

One pad of 18 x 24in (A2) white all-purpose paper or comparable

Charcoal, pencil, pastel, crayons, markers, pen, oil stick, or any medium that can move without needing to be replenished

Directions

In the same way that you did for continuous line, choose an area near the top of the figure to begin. Invest some time in observing the visual and determining which area lends itself to being fully investigated with a studious line. Is there an intricate pattern or print or any area that is an interesting resource of textural information waiting to be recorded?

Step One

Allow your line to move freely, extending itself to investigate the figure (see Figures 4 and 7) or until it rests on an area that you find intriguing (see Figure 1).

Step Two

Evaluate where to go next or which area might also lend itself to the observant character of a studious line (see Figures 2, 5, and 8).

Step Three

If the intent is to further communicate a pattern or textile on the figure, allow the direction of the studious line to inform the direction of the print or pattern (see Figures 5 and 9).

Step Four

From this point, it would make sense to step back from your drawing, take a breath and then decide what is needed to complete the drawing (see Figures 3, 6, and 10).

Opposite: This illustration of Pope Benedict XVI by Tina Berning for *The New York Times Magazine* uses a studious line to capture the eye.

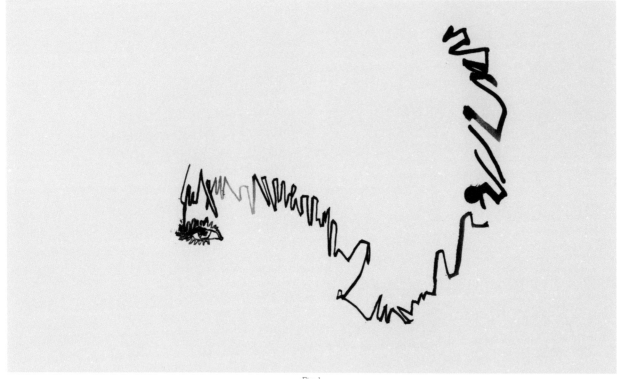

Fig. 1

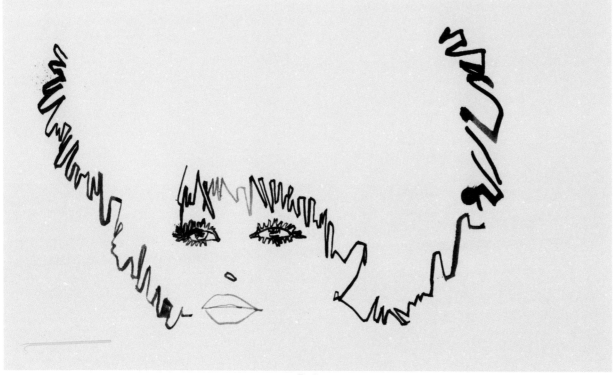

Fig. 2

Fig. 3

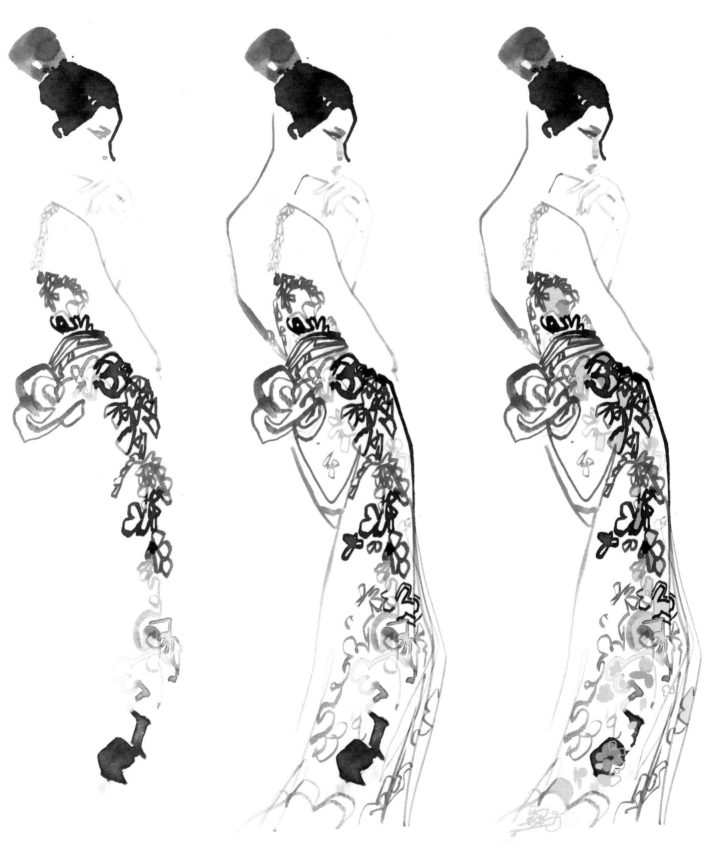

Fig. 4   Fig. 5   Fig. 6

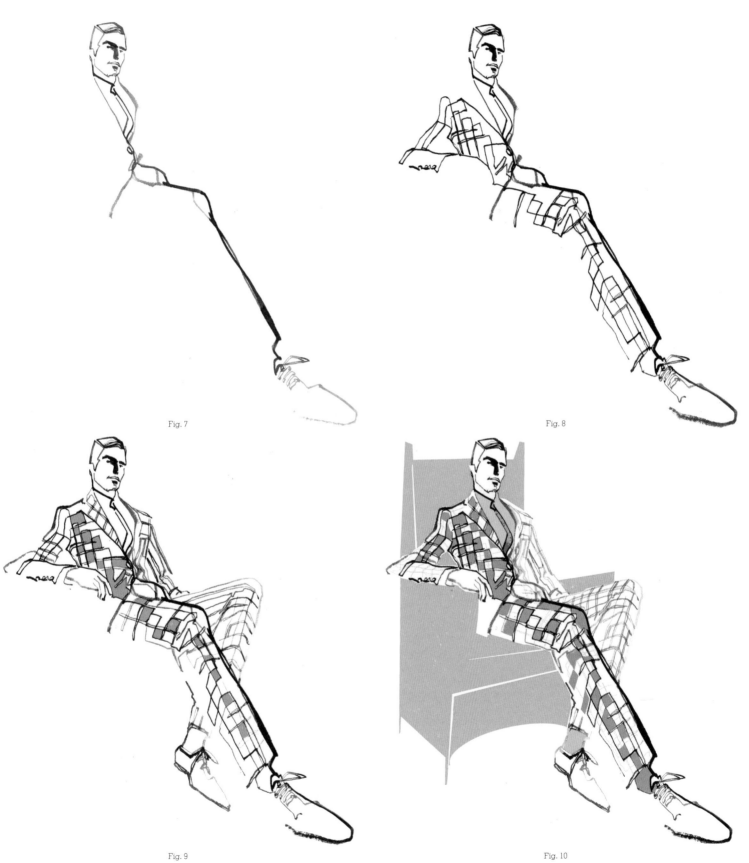

Fig. 7

Fig. 8

Fig. 9

Fig. 10

4.5 Fluid Line

While the studious line is enamored of capturing detail, the fluid line moves to a different rhythm. Carefree, whimsical, and flowing with flair, the name alone signifies the characteristics of a rhythmic line.

A fluid line can be used to describe movement, the folds or drapes of a garment as it responds to the movement or pose of the figure, or the windblown effect of hair or fabric. It can be used to create a whimsical visual regardless of subject matter. All of these features are synonymous with fashion drawing.

You have already witnessed some of the properties of the fluid line in continuous line, where the direction of the line moved in a flowing motion from one point to another (see pp. 94–99). Line quality also gave an indication of fluid lines by using different weights of line to describe space (see pp. 90–93).

Fluid line is a combination of both of these tactics. It flows and also uses a variety of line quality to dance around with an energy and lightness that conveys a sense of spirit and movement.

Despite this cavalier reputation, a fluid line is as knowledgeable as a studious one. But, unlike the studious line, it is usually accomplished with a quick movement of hand to paper. These movements are exacted with a courageous leap of faith and based upon a solid understanding of the figure and form. This confidence allows the line to flow with purpose.

A drawing incorporating fluid lines without any understanding or purpose may serve as a hollow gesture. Anyone can do a drawing with flowing lines without any understanding of why these lines are present, but the effect serves only as camouflage to distract the viewer from the lack of draftsmanship, knowledge of anatomy, or of how to draw the figure.

Preparation

For this exercise, the following supplies are necessary:

One pad of 18 x 24in (A2) white all-purpose paper or comparable

Charcoal, pencil, pastel, crayons, markers, pen, oil stick, or any medium that can move without needing to be replenished

Directions
Observe the figure, evaluating which areas could be communicated with a fast movement of line. Begin your drawing at the top of the figure and use your fluid line with a rapid movement indebted to your knowledge of the figure or visual. It would be prudent to begin the flowing line close to the figure and emanating outward away from the figure.

Step One
If you wish to incorporate a variety of line quality, follow the premise from pp. 90–93 and keep the deepest value of line close to the figure and fade the line as it moves away (see Figures 1 and 3).

Step Two
This line can also be used as a means of whimsical stylistic expression (see Figures 2 and 4).

Step Three
Use the fluid line to accent and give further movement to an area such as the hair (see Figure 5).

Step Four
Once complete, revisit the drawing and add further fluid lines or details to communicate the visual (see Figures 2, 4, and 6).

Opposite: Fluid line is used here to caricature the two Afghan hounds and portray the girls' hair. The best companion for line is a shape. The solid black and white shapes of the figures accentuate the fluidity of the line, which lends an air of grace to the illustration.

4.5 Fluid Line

Fig. 1

Fig. 2

4.5 Fluid Line

Fig. 3

Fig. 4

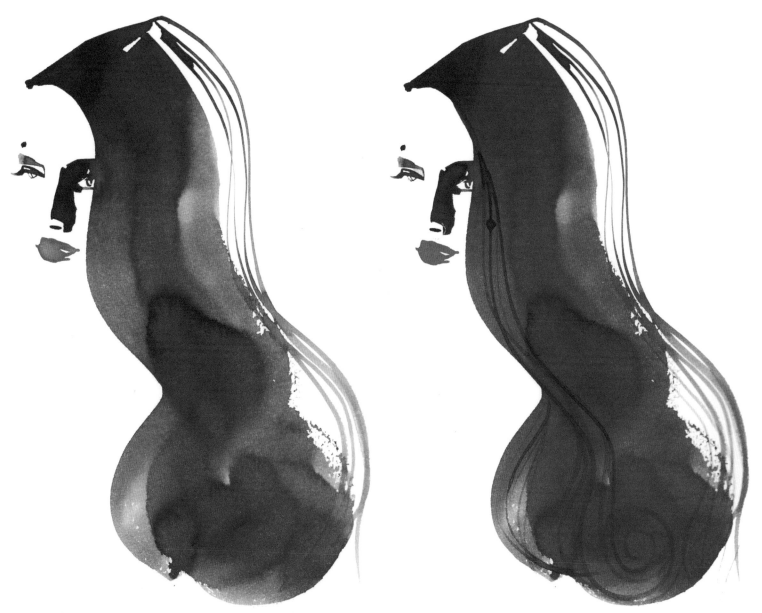

Fig. 5

Fig. 6

Assignment

The aim of this assignment is to reinforce the various exercises that you have completed so far in this book. There has been a lot of information to process, and an ideal way to document your knowledge of this information is to do a series of drawings that enables you to recap the ideas presented in each chapter. Incorporating this information onto one sheet of paper will also prove invaluable to you as a means of charting your progress. It is also a visual resource showing you how observation and thought can guide your drawings.

Preparation

For this exercise, the following supplies are necessary:

One pad of 18 x 24in (A2) white all-purpose paper or comparable

Charcoal, pencil, pastel, crayons, markers, pen, or oil stick

Directions

Onto a large sheet of paper, draw a frame 18in wide x 13½in high (46 x 34cm). Divide this frame into 8 smaller frames of 4½in wide x 6¾in high (11 x 17cm).

In order to fill each frame, you will be required to use your knowledge and command of the vocabulary of shape and line. It is most beneficial to fill in each frame one after the other in one sitting. Examine each drawing as you proceed and compare it to the previous drawing. Push the opposition factor in each drawing to make each completely different.

Frame 1
Draw a figure in strict straight lines.

Frame 2
Draw a figure in straight and curved lines in three shapes.

Frame 3
Draw a figure in five to seven shapes. Think of mapping, using the idea of a black shape that helps describe the visual.

Frame 4
Draw two figures, one in the foreground and one in the back or middle ground in gray and black values. Compose the figures limiting the number of shapes and use the premise of straight and curved lines to contrast the differences between the two figures.

Frame 5
Starting from the upper left-hand corner and working into the lower right-hand corner, do a continuous-line drawing.

Frame 6
Draw a figure using a negative, a black, and a gray value shape. Include an area of continuous line.

Frame 7
Color in this box with a neutral color or paste in a piece of gray paper. Draw the light values on the figure in white. Use a black shape to hold the figure.

Frame 8
Do a drawing of the figure that combines at least three or four of the previous exercises.

1	2	3	4
5	6	7	8

Note:
All of the exercises in this assignment incorporate the premise of composition as an essential component; cropping and the positioning of the figure should be considered.

The use of a model is ideal. If this is not practical, however, a small mirror can suffice and a series of self-portraits can substitute for the model.

Chapter Five
Composing the Figure within an Environment

The illustration visible in today's fashion lifestyle market is driven by concept, style, and composition based on text, promotion, or mood. Although the market may occasionally incorporate an image of a single figure to promote a product or clothing, or to illustrate an article, the format of a loosely drawn single figure captured in a wash and floating in a space and framed by type is now rarely seen.

Whether advertising a luxury cruise, a campaign promoting jeans in an urban location, or using a surrealistic approach to conceptualize an illustration for a website, most illustrations for the fashion lifestyle market will incorporate something other than the idealized single figure.

So far, we have investigated the properties and specific characteristics of the figure using shape, line, and value with selectivity as the guiding light. We have also on occasion introduced the idea of composition, whether drawing the figure in five shapes or observing the figure in a structured frame. It is now time to utilize this information and to incorporate some of the ideas of verticals, horizontals, and diagonals to help enhance the composition and to place the figure in the environment. Foreground and background graphic elements will be introduced as well as using value to create a sense of depth.

Composition

Take a look around you. You are in an environment; an environment composed of shape, line, values, texture, verticals, horizontals, diagonals, and so on. Most importantly, you are a shape within a shape surrounded by other shapes. Creating a composition involves communicating various elements as shapes and configuring those shapes together to form a whole.

In essence, you have been working on your compositional skills since the word "shape" entered your drawing vocabulary. Whether you realized it or not, you have been making compositions throughout this book; you have been doing this while observing and analyzing the figure in terms of shapes and then selecting specific shapes to construct that figure.

Now we will place the shape of the figure within a framed shape and accentuate that shape by using selectivity and some of the principles of composition in choosing shapes to complement the figure.

There are several compositional tools that you can use to help you arrange your shapes: symmetrical or asymmetrical composition; the rule of thirds; the use of scale, repetition, and pattern; positive and negative space; and color and value. These will all work alongside the use of verticals, horizontals, and diagonals that will be explored in the final part of this chapter. Incorporating all these principles opens all sorts of possibilities to create an interesting visual. It is your movie, so to speak, and you are the director composing the frame. The possibilities are endless.

Perspective

The first principle to help in composing the figure in an environment is linear perspective. There are three variations of perspective: one-, two-, and three-point.

To incorporate perspective into any composition, it is essential to first establish a horizon line in the layout. This line is the equivalent of the viewer's eye level. Visualize this horizontal line as the line in a landscape where the land meets the sky. The point on the horizon line where objects receding into space seem to vanish is called, of course, the vanishing point. The number of vanishing points indicates the type of perspective; hence, one-, two-, and three-point perspective.

5.1 One-Point Perspective

The simplest method of placing a figure in a space is one-point perspective, where there is one vanishing point on the horizon line. All lines that are parallel to our central line of vision as it recedes into space will converge at an established vanishing point. Picture a set of railroad tracks that begin as two separate parallel lines and appear to merge as they meet at the vanishing point.

Directions

This exercise is not unlike the one for line quality (see pp. 88–89), where we placed three figures into one frame in the foreground, middle, and background. Here the technical use of one-point perspective will you give you further insights into what gave those compositions a sense of depth.

Step One

Draw a frame and divide it in half horizontally with a horizon line. Place a dot, to represent the vanishing point (VP), in the center of the horizon line (see Figure 1).

Step Two

From the vanishing point, draw four diagonal lines to the corners of the frame (see Figure 2).

Step Three

Draw a framed square around the VP and have the edges of the square line up with the diagonal lines extending from the VP. You now have a simple room with a floor, ceiling, and two walls (see Figure 3).

Step Four

Divide the rest of the space up using additional guidelines that extend from the VP (see Figure 4).

Step Five

Designate the floor space by coloring in this area (see Figure 5).

Step Six

Using the guidelines, start to decorate the room. Begin by placing shapes in the foreground. Starting with the wall space, draw a rectangular shape that would represent the edge of a framed painting inside the guidelines. Color this in a dark hue (see Figure 6).

Step Seven

Extend the edges of this frame into the background, again using the guidelines to help you. Color this area in a lighter tone of the color you used for the outside frame (see Figure 7).

Step Eight

Now put a table into the composition. Since the painting comes to the edge of the room, set the table against the other wall a bit farther back from the foreground. Following the same format as the painting, first put in the front edge of the table. Using the guidelines, draw in the top of the table, extending it so that it recedes into the background (see Figure 8).

Step Nine

Then add the back legs of the table. Initially you can add as many guidelines as you like to place shapes into a composition. However, to avoid having too many lines, simply add them as necessary to extend a line to the shape you are placing in the frame. In this case, the front legs of the table do not line up with any of the guidelines. To know how to place the back legs correctly, draw a guideline from the bottom of the front of the table legs to the VP and use this as the guide to place the back legs of the table (see Figure 9).

Step Ten

Now we can start to add figures into the environment. Place a full figure in foreground, and attempt to have it overlap the painting or table to give an additional sense of space (see Figure 10).

Step Eleven

Now place another figure farther into the space to companion the foreground figure. Note the position of the foreground figure and where the horizon line meets the foreground figure, somewhere around the hip line.

Assuming that the second figure is of the same height and measurements as the foreground figure (in this case we will clone the foreground figure), reduce the size of the cloned figure and position it on the horizon line close to the foreground figure, right by the hip line. If you are coloring this figure, color it with a lighter tone of the foreground figure (see Figure 11).

Step Twelve

The addition of a third figure farther into the space gives the impression of an even deeper room. Again, position the figure with the hip line close to the horizon line. Use a color that is one tone lighter than that of the second figure (see Figure 12).

Note:
Make sure that any element or form that you add into the layout is on the same eye level and plane as the rest of the elements in the composition. You do not want to create an awkward composition by placing a figure seen from a high eye level into a perspective that is developed from a low eye level.

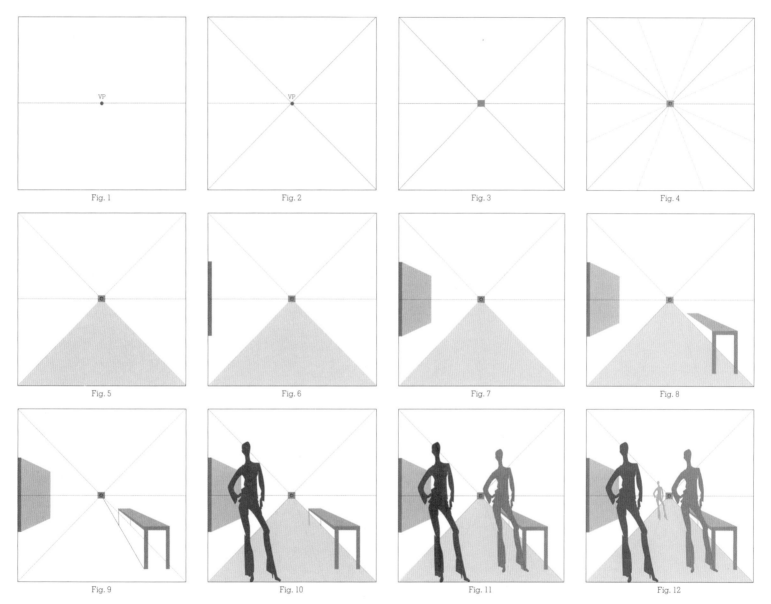

Fig. 1

Fig. 2

Fig. 3

Fig. 4

Fig. 5

Fig. 6

Fig. 7

Fig. 8

Fig. 9

Fig. 10

Fig. 11

Fig. 12

Directions

Two-point perspective incorporates an angular view where the lines receding into space converge at two separate vanishing points on the horizon line. Imagine standing on a street corner and looking down each street converging at that corner. The street ends would each represent a vanishing point (VP).

Step One

Draw a frame and divide it in half with a horizon line and mark two vanishing points at the far ends of the horizon line. Divide the horizon line in the center with a vertical to establish the viewer's central line of vision (see Figure 1).

Step Two

Mark the central vertical line with two points, one at the top and one at the bottom. Draw guidelines from the two vanishing-point dots to the marked dots on the central vertical line. You should now have a diamond shape (see Figure 2).

Step Three

Extend additional guidelines from the vanishing points to the middle central line (see Figure 3).

Step Four

Designate a floor space by coloring in this area (see Figure 4).

Step Five

Now imagine that this is an art gallery. Using the guidelines, much as you did in the one-point exercise, begin to fill the gallery wall with artwork. Choose one wall space and, beginning with the foreground, add in some simple shapes to mimic the shapes of canvases (see Figure 5).

Step Six

Balance the other gallery wall by adding some sculptures. Overlap the artwork to give it an additional sense of depth. Note that even though the sculptures are of different dimensions, they are still positioned using the guidelines as they recede in space toward the vanishing point (see Figure 6).

Step Seven

How about adding some purveyors of art to inhabit the environment? Begin with a figure in the foreground. Assuming that the gallery viewers are closer in dimension, use the guidelines, as you did in one-point perspective, and be a bit more exacting than you were with the sculptures to position them accurately into the space. Identify where the foreground figure falls on the horizon line—in this case somewhere around the waist—and add a smaller figure and position this figure's waist close to the horizon line as well; it need not be exact, as different poses will need subtle adjustments. Note that the brown figure on the other side of the gallery is smaller in scale, but close in height to the black figure (see Figure 7).

Step Eight

Add more people to the environment using the guidelines (see Figure 8).

Note:
Perspective is not a fail-proof science and as you incorporate and explore the different types of perspectives, you will discover that it may not always seem correct. You would be right in that estimation. Trust your intuition and eye when using these principles and allow yourself the poetic license to adjust and move elements as they are appropriate to your composition.

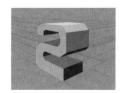

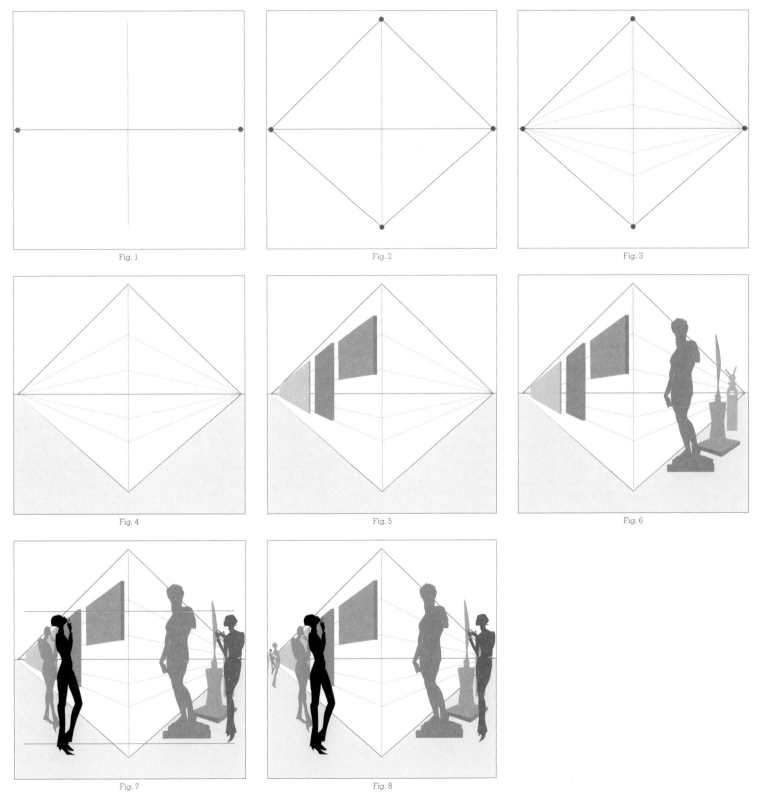

Fig. 1

Fig. 2

Fig. 3

Fig. 4

Fig. 5

Fig. 6

Fig. 7

Fig. 8

5.3 Three-Point Perspective

Directions

Three-point perspective uses and exaggerates a vantage point that is seen from either above or at ground level: a bird's-eye view, or a frog or worm's-eye view respectively. Imagine looking up at a building in a city, or looking down from the top of a building into the street. Three-point perspective creates the illusion of objects that recede to the right and left as well as either upward or downward. In addition to the two vanishing points, as demonstrated in two-point perspective, there is a third vanishing point that is far above or below eye level.

120 We begin again by establishing the horizon line. In this example, this exercise will be based on a viewpoint from below (ground level rather than eye level).

Note:
For the purposes of demonstrating the vanishing points, all of the vanishing points were visible in the framed space. In reality, these vanishing points will probably be far in the distance, beyond and outside of the given framed space.

Note continued:
In the exercises shown, all of the vanishing points were centered to demonstrate the different perspectives. Depending on your viewpoint and eye level the VPs would usually not be centered and static. Shifting the vanishing point farther off to the side in one-point perspective and varying and contrasting the view of the vanishing points in two-point perspective, (seeing more of one than the other), and shifting all three VPs in three-point, will allow for a more vibrant composition.

Step One

Draw the horizon line lower into the frame and mark two VPs at the far ends. Divide the horizon line in the center with a vertical guideline and mark this with three points, one at the bottom, one midway above the horizon line, and one at the end of the vertical line (see Figure 1).

Step Two

As in two-point perspective, draw guidelines from the horizon VPs to the bottom and midway point on the center line to form a diamond-like shape (see Figure 2).

Step Three

Now we need to establish the vertical vanishing point. To do this, add two additional points to bookmark the bottom center point. From these two lines draw in guidelines to the vertical VP (see Figure 3). Note the three vanishing points in your frame.

Step Four

Start adding in the cityscape. To establish how the guidelines help shape the perspective, add a building in the background. Begin with the center line, using the vertical guideline to lay in the shape of a building. Begin at the top of the VP of the vertical line and, following the guidelines, extend the outline of the building, much as you did in one- and two-point perspective to lay in the outline of the form (see Figure 4).

Step Five

Continuing from the middle-ground shape, add in some buildings to the left and right side, overlapping the center shape, and gradually adding the foreground buildings to the composition (see Figure 5).

Step Six

Color in the shapes from the foreground to the background using the darkest tone for the foreground and the lightest for the background (see Figure 6). If you would like to give the cityscape some definition, add in some dark and light values on the angles of the buildings (see Figure 7).

Step Seven

Place a figure into the cityscape to accentuate the forced perspective (see Figure 8).

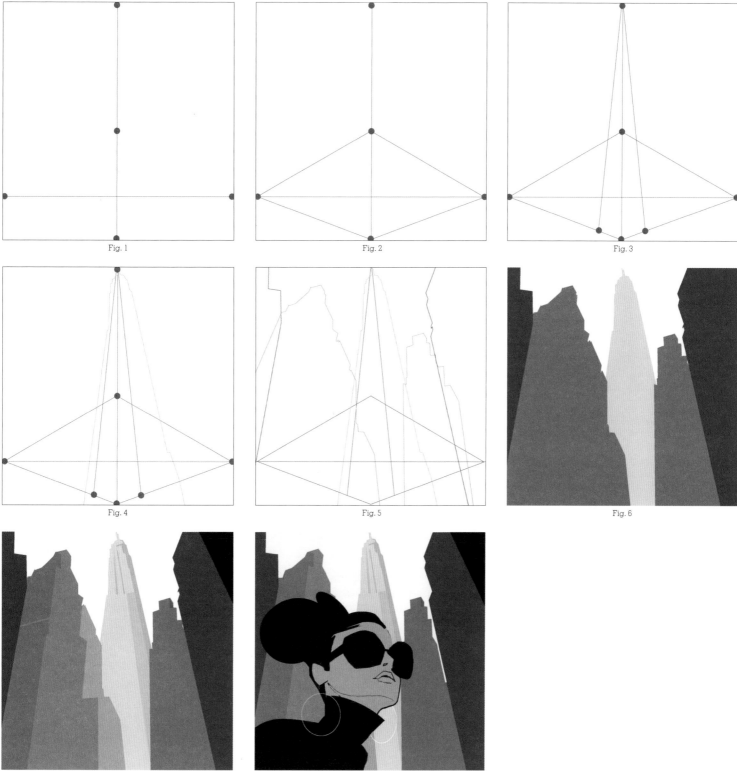

Fig. 1

Fig. 2

Fig. 3

Fig. 4

Fig. 5

Fig. 6

Fig. 7

Fig. 8

5.4 Symmetrical and Asymmetrical Composition

There are two types of composition: symmetrical and asymmetrical. A symmetrical composition is one that is usually centered and has a mirrored effect. In this system, the space is divided in two with evenly spaced shapes that are balanced accordingly, and one side of the composition seems to mimic or mirror the other. This symmetrical composition creates a static presentation that lacks energy (see Figure 1).

An asymmetrical composition, on the other hand, is not bound by any rules confining shapes or forms to specific areas. It is not centered and does not follow rhythm or reason. The elements can be juxtaposed in any manner within the composition, creating an energy that is more dynamic than the static composition of a symmetrical design (see Figure 2).

Fig. 1

Fig. 2

5.5 The Rule of Thirds

Balance is the main driving force behind a successful illustration. There are endless possibilities to creating an asymmetrical composition, and a trained eye and a good dose of selectivity will create one that is both inviting and interesting to the viewer. The freedom extended through an asymmetrical layout does not, however, invite specific principles for designing the space as in a symmetrical design, where everything has a definite placement. Experimentation and knowledge of shapes and their diversity will eventually inform your compositions. There is one principle, however, known as the rule of thirds, that can be used as a guide to assist your eye in designing and positioning the elements within your composition.

We saw in the previous section on symmetrical and asymmetrical composition how the placement of objects or forms can affect the dynamics of that composition. The principle behind the rule of thirds is that by placing elements slightly off-center you will create a more interesting composition that is more attractive to the eye. Just as drawing a frame enables you to be conscious of the space you are creating within it, drawing a grid that divides the picture plane into thirds allows you to place the forms off-center and realize how to push the exaggeration when moving the forms around in an asymmetrical composition.

Figure 1 illustrates how the composition is not utilizing the space to create variety. The figure is centered and the colored wall echoes the figure and divides the frame in half. The sofa and table occupy the horizontal midsection and the lights, although in the top tier of the grid, are positioned in the center of that tier.

Now compare Figure 1 with Figure 2. In Figure 2, the figure, although still occupying much of the middle grid, is off-center, occupying both the first and middle frames of the grid. The figure is also positioned closer to the bottom tier of the grid rather than dead-center as it was in Figure 1. The colored wall has almost been pushed out of the middle frame and creates a dynamic contrast with the negative space that now monopolizes the frame. The sofa has been positioned farther into the bottom tier, while the table is now pushed farther into the middle left of the frame and behind the figure. The lights, in contrast to Figure 1, have been cropped and extend only partway into the upper tier of the grid. The idea is to not be repetitive with your positioning of the elements; use the grid as a rough guide to train your eye to be visually aware of positioning and spacing.

Fig. 1

Fig. 2

5.6 **Scale**

The principle of scale (playing one size against another) can be useful in creating a composition that is unique. This allows each shape to retain its own individual characteristics that work to complement those of other shapes. Exaggeration is essential to create great graphic compositions. If you are going to make the effort to play one shape against the other, why not push it to its limit. Either exaggerate it, or don't bother, that is my feeling; it is much easier to go the distance and then pull back than to play it safe and inch your way out, gradually increasing the scale. If you are entertaining the idea of creating a dynamic composition then playing it safe is not an option. Scale is just such an opportunity.

Look at Figures 1, 2, and 3. In Figure 1, the skater and the trees are similar in scale. In Figures 2 and 3, the skater and the trees were enlarged or reduced in an exaggerated method to create a spatial and visual dynamic. Scale is also another method to communicate space and depth. Scale and exaggeration equal the unexpected and the unexpected keeps the viewer interested.

Fig. 1

Fig. 2

Fig. 3

5.7 Positive and Negative Space

A composition is a sum of its parts, and that includes the areas not occupied as well as those that are. The negative spaces should be considered as important as the positive ones.

Graphically, the fewer elements or shapes you have to work with, the more important those elements become. Be attentive in how you push, pull, and exaggerate all of the shapes in the composition. The goal is to entertain the eye by keeping it interested, and redundancy and similarity will not achieve this goal. In Figure 1, the positive and negative shapes seem balanced. Now observe the variety of the negative shapes in Figure 2 and how they each have a unique character and personality.

126

Fig. 1

Fig. 2

5.8 Repetition and Pattern

Another method you can use to entertain and seduce the eye of the viewer is to use repetition or pattern in a composition.

The use of repetition or pattern allows for a harmonious design in the composition. A repeated use of a shape, line, texture, or value creates a visual rhythm that allows the eye to move or bounce over the work. Not a bad way to seduce the viewer. Repeating a similar shape or element is defined as repetition—think of a flock of birds. The repetition of the same graphic element is generally recognized as a pattern—think of a textile repeat or design. Figure 1 uses the repeated motif of the chairs to create a rhythmic pattern that flows through the composition. In Figure 2, chairs are used in a repeat pattern to form a backdrop for the repetition of figures in the foreground.

When introducing a pattern into an illustration, think of the illustration as a whole—think shape. Shape is the key to adding a pattern or texture. If the composition does not have an interesting play of shapes then the patterns will not accentuate the illustration. Think about composition and how the visual is divided into various shapes—large, small, positive, negative, and contrasting. Add the patterns to those shapes that seem best suited to complement them. A composition devised of multiple patterns can be intriguing, but the eye will eventually need a rest stop. Attempt to keep an area devoid of pattern to allow the eye to rest. Keep in mind that the absence of a pattern in one area can accentuate and complement a pattern in another. Patterns should be incorporated to enhance the main focus of the illustration, the figure, or visual, and should not overwhelm the subject.

Fig. 1

Fig. 2

5.9 Value and Color in Perspective

As you have witnessed, there are numerous ways to create the illusion of space and depth in a composition: using scale to indicate something large in the foreground and something small in the background; overlapping of forms—placing one object in front of the other; cropping of large objects outside of the picture plane; and, of course, linear perspective. Value, color, and their placement in the composition can also indicate depth and space.

Atmospheric perspective describes how the atmosphere affects the appearance of an object in space. The clarity of an object receding in space is affected by the layers of air, moisture, dust, and pollutants that act as a filter to veil the appearance of the object. Objects closer to the viewer are distinct and contrast strongly with the background; objects receding into space begin to lose their contrast with the background. This happens because the strong, bright colors in the foreground become less saturated and begin to mimic the value and color of the background, becoming dull with a blue-gray cast. Sound familiar? We were first introduced to this idea in line quality, where strong, dark, clear lines indicated the foreground figure and faint, pale, light lines dictated a figure in the background. Same premise. In the same way, warm colors also advance toward us and cool colors recede, so bright colors work best in the foreground and cooler colors in the background.

Compare Figures 1, 2, and 3. Observe the differences between each and how the use of value and color seem to pull and push the shapes into the foreground and background. Look at the placement of value and the use of atmospheric perspective. Is one more successful than the other? If so, can you analyze the reasons why?

Figure 1 inverts the idea that warm colors come forward and cool colors recede. The two figures are mostly colored in cool blues and purple; this is incongruous with the warm acid green of the building in the background on the far right, which seems to be pushing for attention and wants to come forward.

Figure 2 seems more natural. As they should be, the cool colors are mostly in the background and the warm colors have rightfully taken up residence in the foreground figures on the skin and suit.

Figure 3 is primarily a study in how value affects depth. Still respectful to the premise of warm and cool colors, this figure uses the theme that the darkest value is closest and becomes paler as it recedes in space. Both Figures 2 and 3 work to communicate depth; however, Figure 3 exaggerates the premise of value (what is closer will be deeper in value) more than Figure 2.

Note how in Figure 3 the foreground figure's suit is the strongest value and contrasts sharply with the background; every form behind this shape decreases in value as it recedes into the landscape, escalating with the background building on the far left, which seems to disappear into the skyline.

Fig. 1

Fig. 2

Fig. 3

5.10 Diagonals

Creating an interesting composition with a figure in a given space relies not only on the position or pose of the figure but also on *balancing* elements in the drawing that accentuate the shapes in the space and complement the positioning of the figure. If the figure is the centerpiece of the art then the surrounding shapes should enhance and complement that centerpiece.

Opposites attract, as we have seen in the previous chapters, and it makes perfect sense to use a vertical to complement a horizontal. Combining verticals with horizontals will elicit a confident, stable composition, as we saw demonstrated in the rule-of-thirds figure (see p. 123). Diagonals, on the other hand, contribute to a layout that has a visual sense of movement created by the opposing directional lines and shapes.

The use of diagonals will help create a dynamic composition, whether alone or combined with a horizontal or vertical shape. When in doubt, use a diagonal format to give action and energy to what would otherwise be a static layout. Playing diagonals against each other allows the eye to move through the space. The key is to recognize the diagonal and emphasize the slant by exaggerating the direction and using an opposing diagonal to further accentuate the movement.

Compare Figure 1 to Figure 2. Both seem to have a sense of movement due to the background diagonal lines. But which layout has a more dynamic feeling of that movement? Figure 2 uses the vertical position of the traveler and pushes that vertical into a diagonal slant. Exaggerating the diagonal direction of the background lines emphasizes this slant. Together, this push and pull of both the figure and the background create a tension that is visually more dynamic and seems to communicate the traveler's movement through the airport terminal.

Fig. 1

Fig. 2

Assignments

Assignment 1

Draw three frames:

A. A square
B. A tall, vertical rectangle
C. A long, narrow, horizontal rectangle.

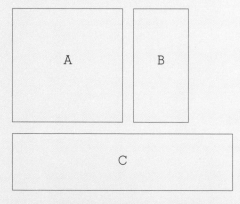

Begin with the square frame. Observe the shape of the frame.
Think of how best to nurture an interesting graphic to move
the eye using the following elements:

1. a road
2. a mountain range
3. a cactus
4. a bird
5. the sun.

These elements should be contrasting in shape and character.
The elements also can be used to fulfill the various premises
of line, shape, and value. Incorporate as many of the principles
of composition as possible: scale, diagonals, repetition, perspective,
and positive as well as negative space should be considered.
Repetition would necessitate multiplying one of the elements. You
can also think about designing your layout using the rule of thirds.
Be conscious of exaggeration and the placement of elements
in the foreground, middle, and background areas of the layout.

Once the square frame is complete, turn your attention to the
tall, vertical frame and incorporate the elements into this space.
Observe the layout and characteristics of the elements in the first
exercise and be conscious not to repeat the style, characteristics,
or layout of those elements in the second frame.

Repeat the process into the narrow, horizontal frame.

Assignment 2

Continue to challenge your eye and knowledge by creating
diverse frames within which to create a composition. Create five
elements of your own and compose those elements into the spaces
you created. Begin to create compositions that reflect the fashion
or lifestyle market. You could choose five or more elements that
are fashion-oriented and create a composition using the principles
as above to place those elements into the space. Consider using
some of the ideas of composition outside of the usual framed space.

Assignment 3

Do a portrait of a celebrity. Use the idea of incorporating just five
shapes or elements into the portrait. Use the outside contour
drawing of the celebrity to compose the five elements. Because
the elements are essential to communicating the celebrity, your
freedom of placement will be limited; however your selection
and choice of rendering of those elements are only as limited
as your imagination.

132

Passages is an illustration created with brush combining ink and color dyes on watercolor paper. The play of positive and negative shapes defines the figures, while the incorporation of accident and chance in the application of the ink gives the illustration a sense of depth and movement despite the absence of line.

Chapter Six
Media

"The medium is the message."
Marshall McLuhan, philosopher, educator, and media guru

Although McLuhan may have been referring to the medium of broadcasting, this statement resonates with the artist as well. The medium chosen to communicate the illustration will also communicate your vision and style.

It is a fantastic feeling to know the basics of a medium and how to control and manipulate it. Having the command of several media will further your proficiency and give you options to change the look of your work. Eventually, using various media will become second nature to you.

Being prolific is a necessity to succeed as an illustrator in the contemporary market. Nothing lasts forever, especially in a market driven by fashion and trends, where last season's "Ins" are on this season's "Out" list. The ability to adapt and change in a capricious climate is as important as developing a unique style. Change is essential; one method of nurturing change and reinventing and rejuvenating your work is to explore a different medium.

Encourage yourself to invent ways to look anew at your work and develop practices that force you to create the work in a method foreign to that with which you are familiar. That is important. If you are adept at drawing, start painting; if you always begin your illustration with the foreground, begin with the background. Change your palette; choose the complements of the colors you ordinarily use. Acknowledging your pattern of working and then changing your pattern will positively influence your work.

The same holds true for exploring media and finding new ways to incorporate them into your work; combine media, change papers, canvas, or surfaces to work upon, invent or create surfaces, draw and paint with balsa wood, sponges, or found items—above all, explore.

In this chapter we will explore wet media, including brush and ink, gouache, watercolors, dyes, and dry media, including charcoal, graphite, pastel, and collage. Finally, we will look at media that defy these categories and discuss Adobe Photoshop and Adobe Illustrator. A recurring theme throughout this chapter will be the idea of experimentation and practice. Try using any of the exercises given in this book to practice using the different media.

Brush and ink on hot pressed paper.

Brush and ink on cold pressed paper.

Sumi brush and ink on soft pressed paper.

Brush and ink on ink-wash background.

6.1 Brush and Ink

Brush and ink is a natural combination capable of producing a variety of effects. Traditionally, brush and ink is associated with the art of sumi-e painting, a Japanese technique using a bamboo brush with natural hair (a sumi brush) and black ink to create quick line paintings with the addition of a gray tone mixed by adding water to the black ink. Selectivity guides the eye, allowing the artist to use an economy of line and tone to create the image.

There are many kinds of brushes, inks, and papers available. Other brushes, which are discussed in the watercolor and dyes section (see pp. 144–145), can be used as well to elicit different effects. Inks are not limited to black; they come in different colors that can be mixed and diluted with water to create an infinite range of transparent color washes to accentuate the economy of line. The type of paper you use will affect the outcome of the illustration. The ideal paper for this wet medium should be absorbent to soak up the medium and not have it rest on the surface. A cold pressed paper (textured) is preferable to one off a hot press (smooth), as a textured paper will hold the ink better. Think of ironing a shirt and how heat smoothes the creases and wrinkles; the idea is the same behind the press of paper. The weight of the paper is another factor; the heavier the weight, the thicker and more absorbent the paper.

Brush and ink is a dynamic and elegant medium that is as versatile as its user. It is immediate and spontaneous.

The use of a brush with a wet medium depends on confident draftsmanship and a fearlessness to trust your eye. The beauty of brush and ink is its spontaneity. The sweep of a brush stroke will create a definite mark; it is important to explore all of the possibilities of using the brush and its capabilities so it becomes an extension of your eye and vision.

Attempt to develop a rhythmic sense of pressure when using the brush. The versatility of the brush stroke depends not only on the type of brush and the saturation of ink, but on how much pressure is applied when making a stroke. Practice a series of strokes beginning at the top of the page and moving toward the bottom. Acquaint yourself with the brush by repeating the painting strokes in one direction on the paper, attempting to make straight lines with no variation of line. Then attempt to create a variety of line by using pressure by painting a line that is narrow at the beginning point and wider at the end point. Follow through with an exercise that reverses this formula.

Experiment with different brushes and the myriad of textures and line those brushes may create. Begin with a large flat brush to map in the visual and move to a medium brush to restate the visual, concluding with a fine brush to place the detail. Allow the brush to become dry and paint a stroke. Try a wet brush, dry brush, wide brush, thin brush, blunt, sumi, and two brushes at once. Allow accidents to occur and become part of the piece. You can experiment with different inks and textured papers, too.

Be fearless. This medium is not for the delicate or faint of heart. It is a strong medium and needs to be handled as such. Before using the brush, look and think about where you want your line to be placed. Then, without hesitation, dip the brush in the ink and follow through.

Advantages

Bold and dynamic medium

With confidence, its user can create emotion, energy, and flair with one sweep of the brush

Can mimic texture by using different brushes and techniques

This medium is capricious and will differ dramatically in results

Disadvantages

It is an unforgiving medium, especially if using waterproof ink

This medium is capricious and will differ dramatically in results

6.2 Graphite

Graphite, usually contained within a pencil or available as a stick, has a wide range of values from dark to light gray. Softer forms, which are classified as "B," produce darker values, while harder forms, classified as "H," produce lighter values.

Graphite allows for a great sense of depth in your work; the various tones can be layered one on top of the other and it easily adheres to a surface. Graphite is fantastic for line and mark-making, creating textures and fine details.

Explore graphite and its versatility by drawing with pencils and sticks. Use the sharpened point to make lines and the broad side of the stick to create blocks of value. Combine the two techniques and invent new ways to work the graphite. It is very important to discover how the graphite relates to different surfaces and interacts with other media. Since graphite is limited to a gray palette, you will need to explore different methods and techniques to reinvent the medium. You could, for example, invest time in finding out how it might react to a smooth surface, such as vellum, versus a coarse one, such as a gessoed board. You could also see how it might work when combined with a wet medium such as ink or gouache. Take the time to start exploring.

Advantages

Immediate results

Versatile

Can be used in a linear fashion or can be layered to create depth and photorealism

Works on all paper surfaces

Pencils are user-friendly, can be sharpened, shaved, or blunted to create different effects

Adheres to the surface of paper

Disadvantages

Limited to gray scale

Has a metallic shine that reflects light

Can leave a shine when applied too heavily or layered onto other media

Adheres to the surface of paper

Note:
Graphite can leave a residue or particles that may smear over the pristine area of a drawing. Placing a sheet of tracing paper or vellum over the initial drawing and resting your hand on this will keep it smooth. To accentuate the smears and incorporate them into the drawing, use a foam applicator or a small wet sponge or paper towel.

Note:
You can also grind graphite into dust and use this as a medium, or to create a specific effect.

6.3 Charcoal

Charcoal, in contrast to graphite, comes in one value—black. But that black is unlike any other black seen in other media. It is a rich, velvety black that saturates the paper and smears and smudges easily, leaving a powdered trail of residue depending on the softness or hardness of the charcoal. It comes in a variety of grades from soft to hard, and is available in many forms from a thick stick to a fine powder. It can also be used with wet media to achieve different effects. The blackness can be tempered with tools and techniques to create a wide range of values from light to dark.

Charcoal is a rite of passage for most artists; it can be used to communicate energy and for rapid sketching. As you are reading this book, you are probably already familiar with charcoal and its properties. Love it or leave it, charcoal, for all its simplicity, is and always will be synonymous with figure drawing, and has a history of use for work that is fashion-oriented.

Practice line quality exercises with soft and hard charcoal. You can also try smearing it to create the visual or the ghost of the visual and then use hard charcoal to draw and restate the visual. Alternatively, fill an area of the paper with a medium-gray tone of the charcoal and use an eraser to lift off the excess to communicate a visual. Wet it, smear it, rub it, and use it with different papers. See what texture and effects you can create with the charcoal alone.

Advantages

Immediate

Versatile

Works on most paper surfaces, but is best used when paper has some tooth or texture to grab the charcoal

Can create unlimited textures and effects

Can be used on top of an underpainting of gouache, acrylic, or watercolor to build up the substance of the artwork

Works just as well creating line as solid areas of value

It is a forgiving medium and can usually be erased and reapplied

Can be combined with wet media to paint or create gray washes

Smears easily

Disadvantages

Powder-based and may need a fixative to prevent smudging

Will not adhere to smooth, polished surfaces

Dust and residue can affect cleanliness of the project

Smears easily

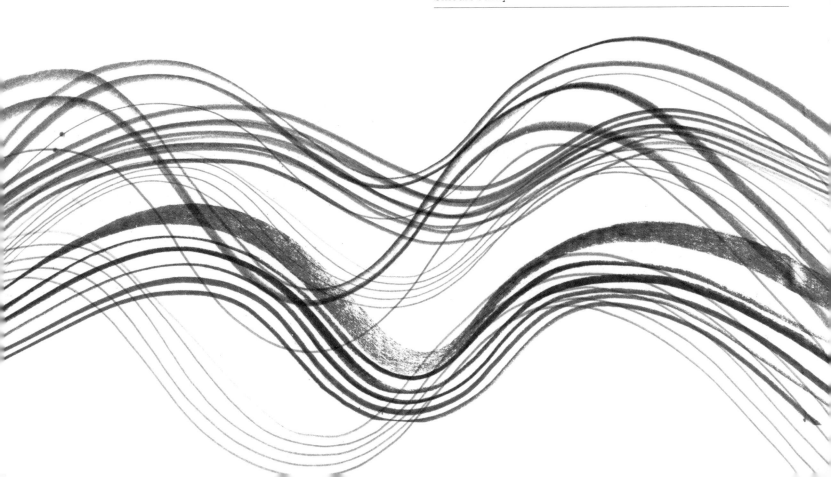

Graphite soft/hard on vellum paper.

Soft charcoal on all-purpose paper.

Hard charcoal on all-purpose paper.

Pastel soft/hard on toned Canson paper.

6.4 Pastel

Pastels are a combination of powdered pigment and a binder. They are available in an infinite variety of hues. They come in the form of sticks or pencils and can have properties from soft to hard. The ratio of binders to the pigment affects the intensity of the color saturation. Soft pastels have the highest concentration of pigment; they are brilliant in intensity compared with hard pastels, which, due to the higher ratio of binder, are duller in color. Soft pastels blend easily, crumble, and need a deep textured surface to adhere to, whereas hard pastels and pencils are more compatible with various surfaces. They can also be built up in layers to create different thicknesses. In contrast to these dry pastels, oil pastels are also available. Oil pastels are bound with the addition of oil and create a rich texture and thickness on most surfaces of paper or canvas.

Pastel can create magic. It is impossible to imagine Degas, Lautrec, or even Monet's Impressionistic artworks without acknowledging the resourcefulness and effect of pastel. Pastel is by nature a medium that can use color to paint as easily to draw. The broad side of the pastel can evoke in one wide stroke the shape of a coat or the turn of a head, while the edge of the pastel can be sharpened with a knife or razor and used to exact the fine detailing of a drawing. Such strokes can be loosely blended and cover a wide area to mimic shadow on the figure or tightly controlled to mimic smoky eye shadow.

In contrast to most methods of applying layers of value—from light to dark—pastel should be layered beginning with media or darks and working toward a layering of lights. A brilliance and intensity in the color can best be achieved with the direct application of the pastel. Blending, although an option, should be used sparingly so as not to overwork the media.

Pastel works well on toned paper. It can also be used over an underpainting to create depth, tone, value, mood, or light. It is a gracious and accommodating medium and seems a natural companion to most dry and wet media. Most dry pastels can also be combined with water to create a colored wash.

Experiment with the pastel by creating a drawing with single, bold strokes, cross-hatching, or solid shapes of color. Play with the pastel to create different textures and effects. Do a loose drawing using five colors only and, once complete, smear the drawing and restate another drawing on top of the smeared one.

You can also try creating an underpainting of three colored pastels in a shaped box on white paper. Once complete, use a brush or wet rag to blend the colors to create a colored ground. Using this colored ground as the medium value, add darks and lights to finish a drawing or a self-portrait.

Finally, do a self-portrait beginning with a dark pastel and then adding light pastels to complete the drawing. Use various papers of different textures to exact different results and don't hesitate to mix the pastel with brush and water.

Advantages

Available in vibrant colors

Versatile

Can be applied in many forms and techniques

Easily applied and layered

Can easily go from transparent to opaque in application

Can be used in a linear way as well as in broad strokes to create mass and tone

Can be combined with wet media to create color washes

Blends to create shadows, layers of color, and textures

Light colors can be applied over dark areas to great effect to create shine or light

Compatible with most media

Breaks easily

Powder-based and can smear easily

Disadvantages

Overworking pastels may muddy the visual

Dependent on paper with tooth and textured, prepared surfaces

Does not adhere to smooth, polished surfaces

Requires the addition of fixative that will dull the colors

Breaks easily

Powder-based and can smear easily

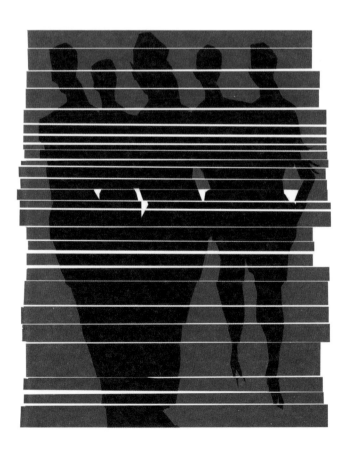

6.5 Collage

Creating work in a collage format allows for unlimited possibilities. In its basic form, collage involves the overlapping and layering on of various flat elements to form a finished visual. The combination of these elements in a compositional format creates a visual narrative. Paper, fabric, newspaper, pages torn from magazines, drawings, and photos, as well as other two-dimensional materials, can all be combined to create the desired effect.

Collage has its genesis in paper, but the advent of digital programs such as Photoshop and Illustrator has nurtured the use of collage for illustration; now there is no limit to what the artist can scan in to create a collage.

Collage is inventive and always a great format in which to reinvent your work. It is dependent on the eye and a graphic sensibility. It forces selectivity due to the laborious nature of cutting the paper to communicate the visual.

Your knowledge of shapes will give you a command over collage. The success of collage depends on composition and a sense of positive and negative shapes. Creating an illustration by collaging cut paper is a good place to begin. If you have the luxury of a model, or a photo, available, then grab four or five sheets of colored paper or pages torn from a magazine, and a craft knife, or scissors if you are handy and patient. Begin as if you were drawing the figure with a pencil and start cutting out the shape of the figure with your tools. Using the balancing-act method and incorporating opposition and positive and negative shapes, do several poses and versions. Use any of the principles of composition discussed in Chapter 5 and lay your cut pieces of paper down to create an illustration. Move the compositional elements around until you have a dynamic visual, and use a glue stick to secure the elements in place. Play with the negative as well as the positive shapes. Allow chance and accidents to occur and use those as the catalyst for a new illustration. Keep an open mind: collage is only as limited as your imagination.

Advantages

Creates an immediate visual

Artist can maneuver the compositional elements around to create various options for the finished illustration

Easy to add or eliminate elements to effect a dynamic visual

Paper can rip easily

Disadvantages

Can be tedious depending on the intricacy of the cut paper or elements included

More accommodating to shape than to linear elements

Small pieces can tear or get lost in the mix

Glue stick can be messy

Paper can rip easily

Opposite: Collage offers limitless possibilities: it can be cut, folded, ripped, overlapped, painted, drawn, or sewn over. An illustrator can include a myriad of images, text, and found objects—anything and everything that is visual can be a part of a collage.

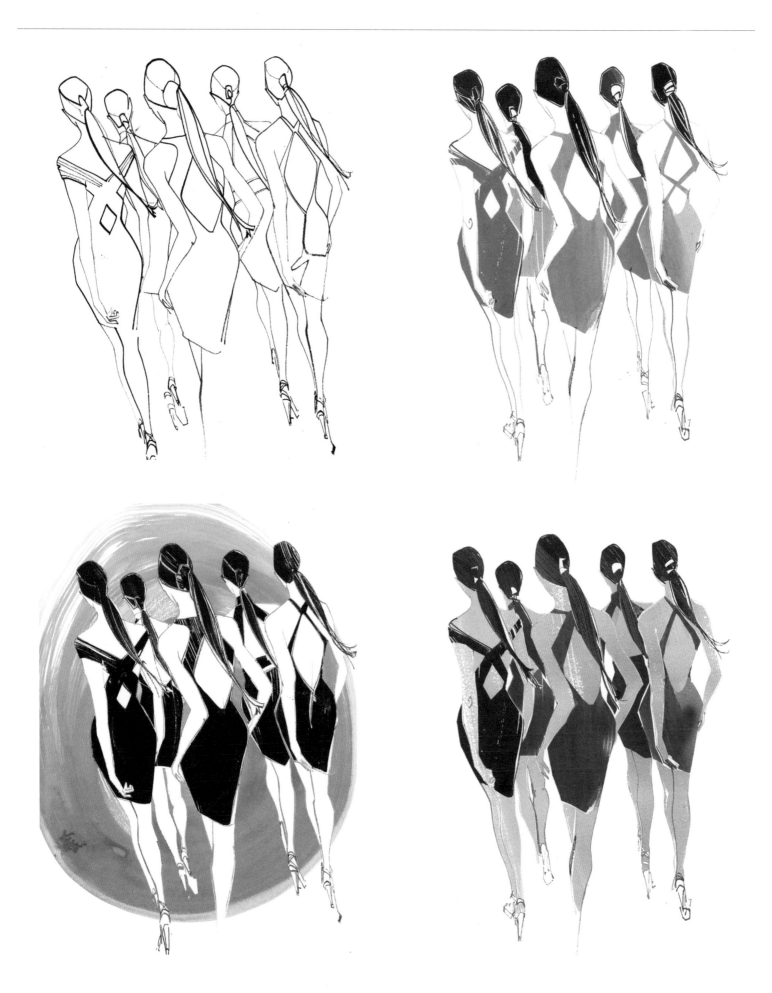

6.6 Gouache

Gouache is a wet medium that comes in tubes. It can be used as a thick and opaque paint or, when watered down, as a light-to-transparent medium to create a watercolor effect. It is usually applied with brushes, but can be used in conjunction with an airbrush or filled pens. It can be used to cover a large area quickly or to add fine detail, and dries to a matte finish. Its ability to be both opaque and transparent and to dry quickly means it is the preferred medium for most illustrators and designers who need a quick and forgiving material that is easy to correct in order to meet deadlines.

Gouache can be applied flat with colors that can be mixed and applied heavily without any streaks or discoloration. Gouache can also be applied thickly with brush strokes that move the paint to create texture.

It is very important to do a test area when using wet media to see how the color differs when dry. The matte surface allows for the artist to combine a variety of dry media with the gouache. Gouache works on most paper surfaces, but is best used on heavier-weight paper to allow a build-up of the gouache without buckling the paper, and with a bit of grip or tooth to allow the paint to adhere to the surface. It is quick, easy to use, and provides great visual results. Its versatility and ability to dry quickly with a velvet-like finish that reproduces well is ideal for most illustrations.

Advantages

Easy to apply and correct

Easy to achieve various textures and results

Dries to a matte finish allowing the addition of other media

Reproduces well

Gouache that has dried can be rehydrated with water and reused

Quick-drying

Water-soluble

Disadvantages

Colors may appear a shade lighter when dry

If applied too heavily it may crack

May dry out in tubes

Quick-drying

Water-soluble

Opposite: Gouache is the medium of choice for most illustrators. It is versatile, can be opaque or transparent, and can be applied with a range of brushes from thin to thick on a variety of surfaces.

144

6.7 Watercolors and Dyes

Watercolors and dyes come in a variety of colors and brands. Watercolor is used as a wet medium and is available either as a thick liquid in tubes, similar to gouache, or as a dry cake of color. Both of these varieties are combined with water. Dyes are similar to ink and come packaged as a wet medium in bottles or jars. The concentrated colors of liquid dyes combine easily with water to make washes of transparent color. The colors of the dyes are vivid and brilliant when applied directly and, like pastels, when applied sparingly can saturate and embellish a piece of paper.

Watercolor brushes, which can also be used with inks and dyes, run the gamut from synthetic to sable, from long to short, and come in many shapes and sizes from the classic round and flat brush to a fan, mop, wash, or angular brush. The scale or size of these brushes varies according to the shape of the brush. They also come in a variety of widths and lengths of hair.

The other component to consider when using watercolors and dyes is the paper. There are many factors involved in the creation and character of paper but, generally, watercolor paper comes in three varieties: hot pressed, cold pressed, and rough. The weight of the paper will affect the properties of these three varieties, and the application of the media on various weights will elicit different results. Hot pressed paper, as we have seen (see p. 135), is smooth, having little grain on the surface. Cold pressed paper has some texture and tooth, which will vary according to the process, while rough is the most absorbent of the three, with a pebble-like surface.

Watercolor is a wonderful medium that is strongly associated with the art of fashion illustration. Layers and washes of color have been used to great effect by artists since the inception of fashion art to convey the essence and sensibility of fashion. The nature of watercolor and dyes allows the artist to create various tones and textures by using washes of color, the layering of transparent color, and painting wet on wet, all with a backdrop of spontaneity, accident, and chance.

Watercolor is used with brushes, and this process lends itself to a fluidity and lightness that can capture the ethereal mystique of fashion illustration. Whereas illustrations created with brush and ink are usually dependent on one tone of black ink, the use of colored dyes and watercolors provides more options to create numerous textures and effects. Incorporating the white of the paper or a negative shape into the illustration will accentuate the color and brilliance of the medium. Whether you use a dry brush or paint wet on wet, or combine your work with Photoshop or Illustrator, these media work well with any dry medium. They can also form a transparent underpainting or color ground that would complement the use of gouache or acrylic. The possibilities are unlimited and usually stunning in effect.

Watercolors and dyes work well when applied lightly and incorporate light and air into the work. Familiarize yourself with the medium by experimenting with different techniques of applying it wet on wet, or dry brush on a wet area, mapping in large areas of color and adding details. Find a simple black and white photo from a newspaper or magazine that has a sharp composition of lights and darks. Position the photo upside down and choose one color of dye or watercolor. Analyze the photo in terms of the dark, medium, and light values. Dilute the color selected to create a monochromatic painting using the deepest saturation of the color for the darkest value and the diluted color for the medium value. The lightest value will be the white of your paper.

Once you feel comfortable using the media, substitute three different colors for the values and continue another painting using three colors to represent the light, medium, and dark values. Begin painting in the shape of the lightest value with the assigned color, then layer in the medium and then the darkest values.

Advantages

Easy to clean

Pan colors travel well and are suited for location painting

Can create many different tones and textures

Tubes of watercolor mix and dissolve easily

Able to stain paper

Unpredictable

Disadvantages

Needs time to dry

Dry watercolor cakes can be laborious to work into a wet medium

Tube watercolor can dry out

Able to stain paper

Unpredictable

Opposite: Watercolors and dyes can create a variety of effects to great purpose. Whether used on hot pressed or cold pressed paper, or anything in between, the wonderfully capricious nature of this medium guarantees that no two results will ever be alike.

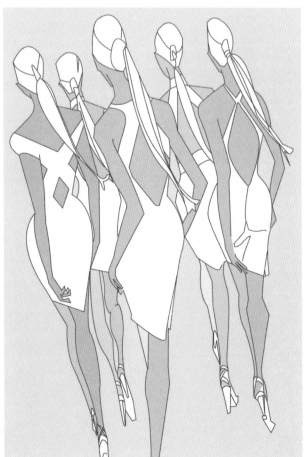

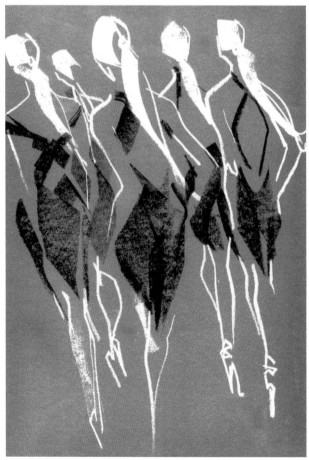

6.8 **Photoshop and Illustrator**

The choice is yours, but what a choice. Two media that defy any categorization of being dry or wet are Adobe Photoshop and Adobe Illustrator. Within two decades, these digital programs have redefined the nature and direction of illustration as well as many other disciplines in art.

Aside from a command of traditional media, illustrators now also need a thorough knowledge of Photoshop and/or Illustrator and use them in their artwork. Solo, or in combination, these digital programs are as essential as charcoal or a brush loaded with ink.

However they are used, the various tools and options in the programs have no limit in their capacity to affect the look and finish of the illustration. Either program has the ability to create original work or enhance traditional work at any stage, from rough sketches to a finished piece.

Most illustrators are devoted fans of Photoshop, which is a bitmap program that uses a pixel-oriented system to modify and edit or enhance an image, while others rely more on Illustrator for its vector-based graphic abilities. Whatever the choice, the majority of artists seem to concur that both programs are essential to each other and work best when combined.

These programs have taken a solid foothold in the world of illustration and have revolutionized the techniques, processes, and the future of illustration. We will examine their impact in more detail in Chapter 7.

Advantages

Options, options, and more options

Digital artwork

Disadvantages

Options, options, and more options

Digital artwork …

Opposite: Photoshop and Illustrator provide infinite options for manipulating and editing work. Photoshop will create a more nuanced effect compared to Illustrator's vector-based technology, which is best used for graphics.

Graphite, ink, and Photoshop.

Ink, gouache, Illustrator, and Photoshop.

Gouache, ink, and paste.

Gouache, ink, and Photoshop.

6.9 Combining Media

Proficiency is important in maintaining a competitive edge in an ever-changing market. Knowledge is power and the better your ability and skill in using the media discussed in this chapter, the better your options will be to create a style that is unique to your vision.

Each medium has a particular characteristic and nuance, but combining them with different methods and techniques will reinvent the medium and your work. Exploration should be the driving force of discovering methods that resonate with your personal style.

Try combining two or more of the media in different exercises in the book. Experiment to combine media, tools, and surfaces to extract a unique illustration. Use a large mop brush, loaded with ink, dyes, or gouache, in conjunction with a detailed brush or graphite pencil; blend pastel with collage; draw with a brush and paint with a tree branch; play with different surfaces to discover how the medium translates and reacts to those surfaces. Seek out other media to use, such as crayons, oil sticks, markers, conté, and sponges, or collage with found items, such as string, wire, or fabric. Incorporate the tools of Photoshop and Illustrator into the process to enhance and stylize the illustration.

Most of all, keep an open mind; don't censure your accidents or mistakes, for one artist's frustration is another's success.

Advantages

Limitless

Disadvantages

None

Note:
Mix it up! Do several pieces in different media and then collage them together, or take the best elements and incorporate them in one piece.

Chapter Seven
The Computer and Illustration

"I never base an image on the merits of a program. Sometimes I have a clear idea of what I want for the final image and other times I play with the image until the unexpected occurs and I am satisfied with the final image. Illustrator is ideal for this type of work, but it is secondary to the idea of line and shape. The work I create is influenced by a solid foundation in drawing with an eye to simplicity."
Carlos Aponte, artist–illustrator

Times have changed. Today the computer is an essential tool to success in the lifestyle market of illustration. The world of illustration is now shaped around access to the Internet as well as the digital programs available to the illustrator. Whether or not you incorporate the programs into your finished work, there is no escaping them.

The principal software programs for illustrators, as we have seen, are Adobe Photoshop and Adobe Illustrator (see pp. 146–147). These programs allow the user to create multiple compositions of work; the infinite variety of options produces an infinite variety of art.

When artists are introduced to using these digital tools, there is a common tendency to use as many options as possible. This can create a visual that is overworked and overshadowed by the modes and options of the programs. These options can be overwhelming and using the idea of selectivity can assist the illustrator in navigating through the programs.

The Internet

The Internet provides an unlimited treasure trove of resources for the illustrator. The options are endless. Websites of every inclination, from directories to reference tools to tutorials and promotion, have profoundly affected the domain of illustration. The Internet has also created a lucrative market for illustration with a vast number of websites that incorporate illustration as a means of promotion, animation, or to provide a graphic complement to the content.

If you are a working illustrator today, then you will most likely be corresponding with your client and receiving and sending artwork as digital files through the Internet. There are many types of file formats. The most universal files used are:

PSD, Photoshop Document (.psd)—the native file of the program that retains all of the information of the file for further editing.

JPEG, Joint Photographic Experts Group (.jpg)—a compressed file that is most commonly used for email and the web.

TIFF, Tagged Image File Format (.tif)—an uncompressed high-quality format ideal for printing.

Each can be saved in different resolutions or Dots Per Inch (dpi), also known as Pixels Per Inch (ppi); 72dpi is ideal for the web and 300dpi is ideal for reproduction.

Shape, Composition, and Selectivity

Although times may have changed, what has not changed is the need for draftsmanship, a trained eye, and an understanding of shape, composition, and selectivity—the foundations of this book. Using these principles will allow you to successfully incorporate programs such as Photoshop and Illustrator into your work. It is extremely important to understand and have a grasp of these digital options and it is nothing less than incredible to see how these options can literally recreate an illustration.

You are probably familiar with this software and realize that these programs generally rely on knowledge of shapes, for example, to select an area to effectively use the numerous tools. Play with the modes, tools, and options as much as you like, but realize that the essence of the work is created from your skill and talent as a traditional artist. Without a foundation in drawing, painting, composition, and selectivity, these tools are at best just tools and will not be used to their best advantage.

Using selectivity and limiting the number of options incorporated into the work will highlight your talent as a traditional artist and aid you in creating an illustration that seems confident and concise. Using composition will allow you to select and order the options available in the software. That essence and your skill and vision are what will give you an edge as an illustrator, marking you out as one who is not dependent on using the program options to make your work but one who uses the options to accentuate your vision.

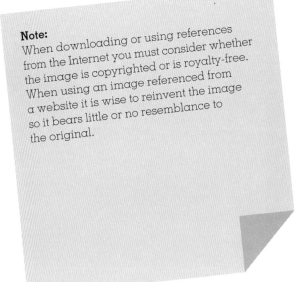

Note:
When downloading or using references from the Internet you must consider whether the image is copyrighted or is royalty-free. When using an image referenced from a website it is wise to reinvent the image so it bears little or no resemblance to the original.

7.1 Combining Artwork with Photoshop

Technology in the digital age has simplified processes and techniques and made the art of illustration run faster and more efficiently. Creating a layout in Photoshop allows the artist to effortlessly edit and move compositional elements. This is particularly useful in today's lifestyle illustration market, where there is often a need to incorporate the figure into an environment.

One of the first steps toward creating an illustration is research. Picture collections and periodicals used to be the main source of research for most artists and illustrators investigating reference for an illustration. The Internet now allows an artist immediate access to files of photo reference, and many sites are created specifically to answer this need. When a reference will not suffice, a digital camera and model can quickly fulfill the same goal.

Research can produce many images to incorporate in a composition. Complex compositions are easily simplified through Photoshop's mode of layers. Think of separate images on acetate sheets overlapping one another. Layering allows the illustrator to move and reposition the images to suit the goals of the composition. A simple method to initiate a layout is to use the foreground, middle, and background principle to position the forms, moving images back and forth until the right effect is achieved.

Like pieces of a puzzle, the components can be put together through software to make a complete picture. However, unlike a puzzle, pieces can be edited and transformed to create many complete pictures.

Directions
In this illustration, each element was created either from life, from references downloaded from the Internet, or from digital photos. The perspective is from that of the audience; therefore, all of the compositional elements had to reflect a worm's-eye view.

Step One
The audience members were drawn from a combination of different web-based references (see Figure 1). The lights were drawn from a digital photo of a fashion show (see Figure 2). The three drawings of the model were drawn from life (see Figures 3, 4, and 5).

Step Two
Each of these elements was scanned into Photoshop and created on separate layers to allow for a variety of movement and compositional options. After exploring different variations of layouts, the final composition opposite was decided upon.

The audience members were positioned in the foreground. The figures were individually positioned into the middle ground of the composition, transformed in scale, and recolored.

The lights were positioned behind the figures, rotated to create a strong diagonal, and lightened to fade into the background, allowing the figures to come forward. Additional audience members were desaturated of color, reduced, and positioned into the far background.

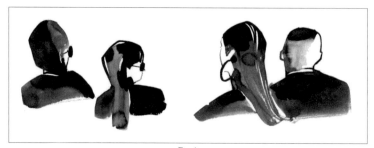

Fig. 1

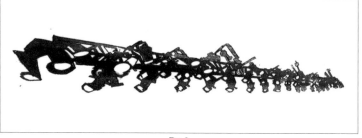

Fig. 2

Fig. 3

Fig. 4

Fig. 5

Illustrator is a vector-based program, ideal for drawing with line. The benefit of using vectors is the ability to change lines and manipulate shapes easily. The lines and shapes are created by anchor points. These are tiny squares that, when connected to each other, can create lines and shapes; four anchor points, for example, can create a square or a circle. Complex images can have hundreds or thousands of anchor points. These anchor points have direction lines within them and the process can be described as a steering wheel that turns the car in different directions. Images can be scanned in and used as reference to be traced over using the vectors, or shapes can be drawn from scratch. Images can be created in layers and the different elements then moved around, as in Photoshop, or drawn as a single image.

The rooster in the image right, by Carlos Aponte, was drawn from scratch, while the tropical plants and the palm trees were drawn first as sketches from reference sites on the Internet and from images in periodicals and then scanned into Illustrator. The image was then assembled in a single layer. Initial loose sketches of the plantain trees were made bold and organic to complement the clean graphics of the rooster. A monochromatic color scheme of tropical greens and blacks was used to balance the illustration and avoid the complexity of images overwhelming the icon.

154

Opposite: Carlos Aponte created this image of a rooster for a promotion for which the theme was flora and fauna. He wanted to create something that was optimistic, fun, and whimsical. Having grown up in Puerto Rico, he associated the image with his childhood and wanted to combine this warm nostalgia with a modern twist. Using Illustrator, but basing his illustration upon a firm foundation of drawing skills and the use of shape, he has created an image that is striking in its complexity of shapes but also in its simplicity.

Note:
As demonstrated by Carlos Aponte's rooster opposite, the vocabularies in this book of line shape and stylization, associated with fashion illustration and drawing, can also be incorporated into other visual disciplines, including graphic design.

7.3 Patterns and Textiles

What a difference a decade makes, especially when it comes to the labor-intensive work of creating a repeat of a pattern to place within an illustration. There are now numerous techniques available through digital software. Any image can easily be transformed into a pattern—copied, pasted, multiplied, reduced, enlarged, colored, and transformed with the click of a mouse or a drawing tablet. The pattern in the image on p.127 was created from the image of the chair also on the same page. The image was reduced, rotated, duplicated, copied, and pasted to form a finished pattern to fill the background.

Above: Bo Lundberg uses shape selectivity to create this illustration. Employing the tools within Illustrator, Bo effortlessly incorporates a mixture of pattern, texture, color, and print to create depth and contrast within a simple silhouette.

Above: Cecilia Carlstedt uses repetition as well as a large shape in her placement of the pattern within the picture plane, employing both traditional and digital skills to do so. The variation of scale and the diagonal direction of the patterns echo the rhythmic nature of the floral patterns in this illustration for Swarovski. The greater part of the pattern and print is centered around the figure and begins to gradate into a linear shape as it moves away from the figure.

158

Chapter Eight
Fabric, Prints, and Texture

Patterns and prints are present everywhere and are intrinsic to lifestyle and fashion illustration. Patterns can be used graphically as a background or simply as a print on clothing. How and where you use them can have a wonderful visual effect and enhance an illustration, as we have seen in Chapter 4 (see pp. 104–105), Chapter 5 (see p. 127), and Chapter 7 (see pp. 156–157).

Prints and patterns are unique. Each one is different. The mixed, flecked colors of a tweed created from a knit fiber, for example, are vastly different from a woven version in wool and different again from a pattern printed on satin or on a sheer material such as chiffon or georgette.

In the same way that there are endless variations of pattern and texture, there are endless solutions to illustrating patterns and textiles. How and what to use to convey a particular material or texture should be up to the individual artist. Experimentation and exploration with media (see Chapter 6) is the best method of discovering which technique resonates with your vision or your style. The one constant to translating a print or pattern is simple—observation.

In this chapter, we will work with organic and flowing prints and patterns and then with structured patterns, identifying the similarities and differences between the two, and looking at how to place each within an illustration. Finally, we will look at working with sheers.

Opposite: Intrinsic to lifestyle illustration is the ability to incorporate pattern and texture into your images, whether as a literal part of the illustration, as in the prints and patterns drawn by Cecilia Carlstedt (top left) and François Berthoud (below right); as a graphic element to add interest to a visual, as in the drawing by Eva Hjelte (top right); or as a decorative element of the illustration, as shown by Bo Lundberg (bottom left).

8.1 Organic and Flowing Prints and Patterns

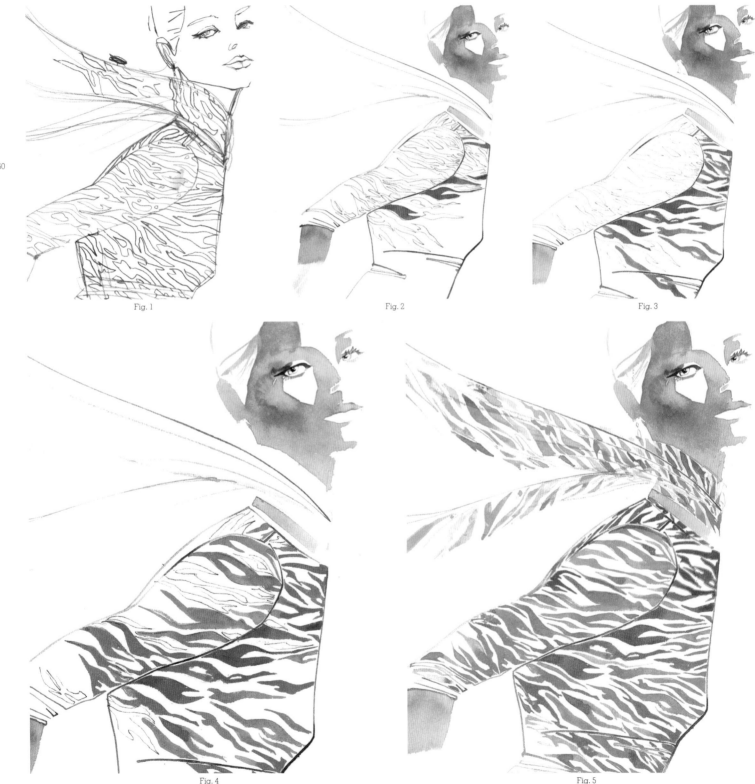

160

Fig. 1

Fig. 2

Fig. 3

Fig. 4

Fig. 5

8.1 Exercise 1: A Simple Colored Pattern

Organic and flowing prints and patterns have a natural rhythm. This rhythm is a result of the repetition of the design elements of the print, which is called a repeat. This repeat creates a seamless balance that allows the eye to move throughout the print. Using a rhythmic flow to position the print into the illustration gives a sense of movement to the illustration, too (see p. 127).

Step One
Start by making a linear drawing of the figure and mapping the print onto the visual. Observe and analyze the pattern of the print—the rhythm, scale, and placement of the various elements within the print in terms of contour and shape. This will allow you to dissect the print and place those shapes into your illustration (see Figure 1).

Step Two
Always begin at the top of the figure. Using your map of the print as a guide, lightly trace the pattern onto your illustration. Follow the natural curves and diagonals of the figure as you place the colors of the print. Decide which area will be the area of movement; in this case the diagonal of the torso was selected to play off of the diagonal of the scarf and arm. Layer in a large or main area with one color. Make allowances for the form of the figure and leave space for additional areas of the print (see Figure 2).

Step Three
Once a movement begins to surface, add in an additional color within the same area. I prefer to erase the pencil line in those areas completed to avoid distraction from the faint pencil lines of the guide (see Figure 3).

Step Four
When the print begins to fill in the major area, start to extend the print out to other areas. It is important to keep some areas open to incorporate spontaneity into the illustration (see Figure 4).

Step Five
Once the major area of movement in the print is painted, start to add pattern into the scarf with confidence and using your knowledge of the rhythm and essence of the print (see Figure 5).

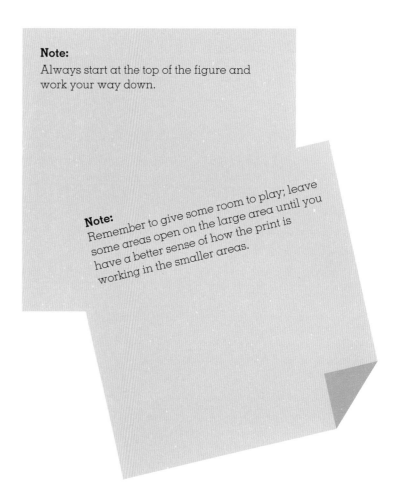

Note:
Always start at the top of the figure and work your way down.

Note:
Remember to give some room to play; leave some areas open on the large area until you have a better sense of how the print is working in the smaller areas.

8.1 Exercise 2: A Detailed Floral Print

Step One

Follow the same directions as above, using the map (see Figure 1) as a guide to place the floral print. Place the larger design elements of the print first followed by the smaller leaves and flowers. Observe the figure and visualize how the print would move across and around the anatomy of the figure to give movement so that the print does not appear flat. Here, the arm in the foreground and curve of the back were selected as areas of movement (see Figure 2).

Step Two

Observe the pattern of color and layer in the lightest color of the floral. It is always easier to go from light to dark and make corrections than from dark to light (see Figure 3).

Step Three

Using the direction of the form, begin to add a second color onto the pale layer. Add some of the additional elements to begin to build the print (see Figure 4).

Step Four

Continue adding in deeper values as you progress through the figure. The highest saturation of color should be limited to the area of movement; areas extending outside of the main area—such as the arm here in the background and the outside line of the back —should not be as prominent (see Figure 5).

Step Five

Continue to add color to complete the illustration. In Figure 6, in order to accentuate the curve of the arm in the foreground area and the curve of the back, that area was defined and saturated with color in contrast to the background arm and the outside line of the back.

Note:
Work from top to bottom each time you add a layer of color or print. This will guarantee a uniform look to the color and balance.

Note:
It is easier to build onto a lighter color than lighten a darker one.

Note:
The highest saturation of color should be reserved for the area of movement in the illustration. Also, use the premise from line quality: what is closer will be deeper and what is farther from the eye will fade.

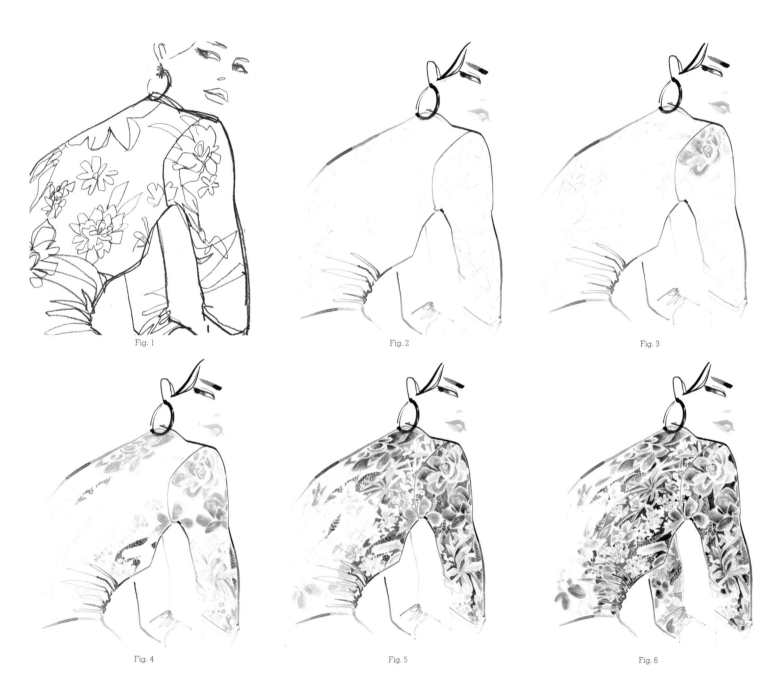

Fig. 1

Fig. 2

Fig. 3

Fig. 4

Fig. 5

Fig. 6

8.1 Exercise 3: An Organic Print

Step One

Organic prints seem to evolve as they move through the figure. In order to retain a sense of spontaneity through the figure, no pencil guide was created for this exercise. Pencil was drawn directly into the illustration following the curve and line of the figure, with a nod to the movement of the skirt and vertical of the bodice (see Figure 1).

Step Two

Use areas of movement to add a ground color. Here the movement of the print and skirt was used to guide the placement of a ground color around the outline of the biomorphic shapes. This color was kept close to the figure and does not extend to the hemline or outside of the main area of interest (see Figure 2).

Step Three

Unlike the previous exercises, here a darker value was placed within the biomorphic shapes. Once the dark value defined the figure, additional ground color was extended outside of the main area of interest (see Figure 3).

Step Four

Finally, add in your medium and lighter values. Here they are blended into the dark area of the print and then float out from the main area of movement (see Figure 4).

Note:
Add some spontaneity to the print; use the map as a guide and allow poetic license and intuition to guide your hand.

Fig. 1

Fig. 2

Fig. 3

Fig. 4

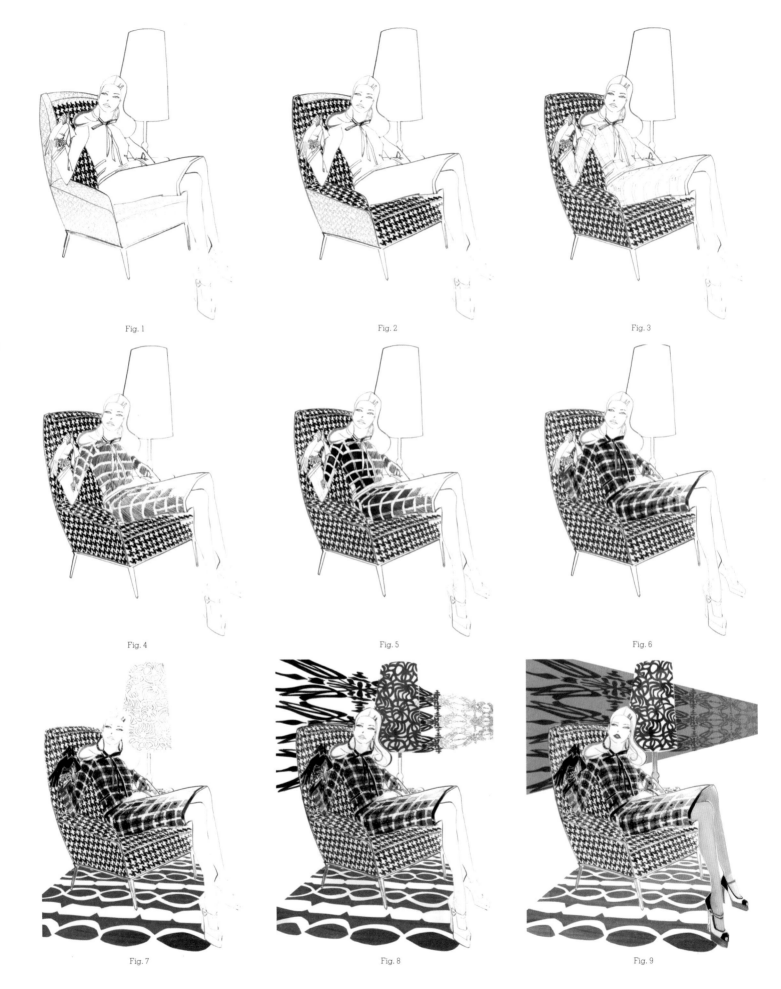

Fig. 1

Fig. 2

Fig. 3

166

Fig. 4

Fig. 5

Fig. 6

Fig. 7

Fig. 8

Fig. 9

8.2 Plaids, Hounstooth, and Structured Patterns

Prints and patterns can also be more structured in nature. Houndstooth, plaids, and checks, for example, are composed in a methodical grid design that is easily applied to your artwork.

These structured prints, as noted in Chapter 5 (see p. 127), can also be used as a graphic component to enhance the illustration.

Aside from careful observation, there is another essential quality an illustrator must have when incorporating prints into an artwork—patience. Knowing when to stop applying the print is just as necessary as following a graphic movement. Structured prints can create a fantastic effect, but can be laborious to apply and tire the eye and hand. Patience in the layering in of the print will affect the outcome of the illustration. To avoid rushing the process, take a break or begin filling in another area of the illustration. Patience has its rewards, and investing time and effort to exact the structured print will create a more dynamic and intriguing illustration.

In this exercise we will use the grid from different kinds of structured prints, including houndstooth and a plaid, to place a structured pattern into a figure and a background environment.

Note:
Some prints can create an optical illusion and it is easy to lose your way in the process of filling them in. If a print becomes too confusing, with similar positive and negative areas, lightly mark the positive area with a pencil as you draw the print as a guide to which areas will be filled in with color.

Note:
If using a wet medium, such as gouache or inks, have enough color of the print mixed to prevent color changes.

Step One
Because of the intricate and repetitious nature of houndstooth, start with a pencil drawing of the pattern mapped onto tracing paper as a guide. This can then be transferred to the line drawing of the actual illustration. Here allowances were made for the dimensional structure of the chair and the way in which the pattern would fill in the different areas. One place to start filling in your pattern could be an area bookending a shape. Here the area framing the figure was chosen and the houndstooth was filled in until the figure was silhouetted by the print (see Figures 1–3).

Step Two
Analyze a plaid into a grid of vertical and horizontal lines. Beginning with the top of the figure, draw in pencil the vertical lines of the plaid, as they would move over the contours of the figure and clothing. Add in the horizontal lines (see Figure 3).

Step Three
Within the grid of pencil lines and, again working from the top of the figure, layer in the blocks of one color of the plaid. Try starting with the lightest in color or value—in this case, the gray areas of the plaid were filled in first (see Figure 4).

Step Four
Layer in the darker area where the vertical and horizontal rows of the plaid meet. This will usually create a deeper value or color as they overlap in this area of the grid. Begin to add some of the smaller rows of the vertical and horizontal plaid (see Figures 5–6).

Step Five
Once the plaid seems complete, begin adding additional design elements. Here elements of the room were added to frame the figure. The carpet anchors the figure, while the pattern of the lamp frames the right side of the figure (see Figure 7). The wall painting is added to complete the composition (see Figure 8).

Step Six
Finally, clean up areas and add in the small details to complete the illustration (see Figure 9).

8.3 Translucent Sheers

The illusion of sheer fabric in an illustration can be charming and elegant and can convey a sense of depth, light, and movement. Whether it is a wind-blown scarf or curtain, at some point you will be asked to impart the feeling of a translucent material such as chiffon or georgette. To achieve this, aside from observation and patience, you will need to add another term to the mix—saturation.

In the previous exercises, the saturation of color was centered in the area of interest of the figure. In this section, we will observe how varying the saturation of color can elicit the illusion of translucency.

Materials such as chiffon, georgette, or tulle have a translucent nature and, when layered over other areas of color or print, will act as a filter, allowing those colors and prints to be visible.

In an illustration, what is visible through the translucent material can be defined by the amount of color saturation (the brightness or dullness of a color), in which the color is either heightened or dulled by the hue of the translucent area. If you were to view a bowl of lemons and limes through the filter of a pair of rose-colored glasses, for example, the green of the limes would appear dull while the yellow of the lemons would intensify in saturation and appear orange. The color of the filter affects the color of the object seen through the filter.

Directions
Follow the same principle of observation as in the above exercises; your focus should be on the shape or area of the material that is translucent. Once the lines of the sheer are defined, lightly pencil in the print or pattern. The line describing the sheer should also be thin and translucent; a hard line would be incongruous given the nature of a sheer material.

Step One
Begin to fill in the sheer material that is not overlapping another color or tone. The translucent area will always be lighter in value than any opaque areas. It is best to work from light to dark in most instances, as it is easier to correct or amend (see Figures 1–3).

Step Two
Add some additional fluid lines to give some spontaneity to the movement of the sheer material (see Figure 4).

Step Three
Begin to fill in other areas of the illustration. This time begin to paint in the darker areas, saving the lighter tone for those areas that are overlapped by the sheer. Keep in mind that the translucent material will act as a filter and, therefore, change the color or saturation of the material seen through the filter (see Figure 5).

Step Four
Once the main areas are complete, begin to add in the small details. To further accentuate the illusion of translucency, exaggerate some of the darker tone that is closer to the lighter tone of the sheer and, if necessary, lighten some of the sheer areas (see Figure 6).

Note:
Use the color of the print to draw in the shape of the print.

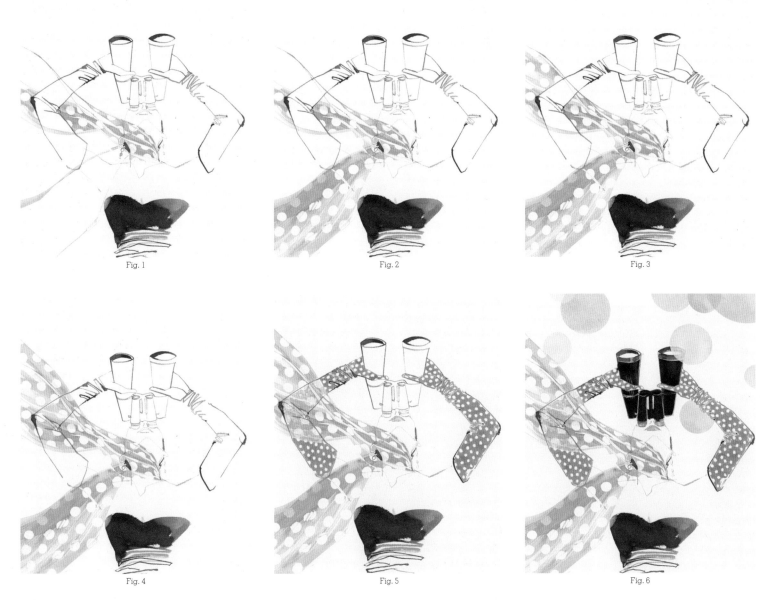

Fig. 1

Fig. 2

Fig. 3

Fig. 4

Fig. 5

Fig. 6

Chapter Nine
Finding Your Voice

"There is a vitality, a life-force, an energy, a quickening that is translated through you into action and because there is only one of you in all of time, this expression is unique. And if you block it, it will never exist through any other medium and be lost."
Martha Graham, dancer and choreographer

There is no proven method or specific technique to teach you how to discover your voice. No one creates a style overnight. Time, experience, and an innate awareness of your particular place in time will nurture the development of your style.

Your environment and taste in music, fashion, clubs, trends, and art will determine your outlook and affect your work. Artists are visual recorders of life. The more exposure we have to different venues, events, and experiences, the richer the resources we have to draw upon. Keep a sketchbook and record everything, everywhere, whenever possible. Don't rely solely on the web for reference; create your own folder of references that reflect your eye and not the eye of another artist. Have available a digital camera and create files of visual reference. Visit art galleries, take a class, be an active participant in life and allow that experience to filter into your work.

Your personal sense of style, fed by your observations, will enable you to choose the words from the vocabulary we have been studying throughout the book—shape, line, value, and composition—that will help create your individual drawing style.

Using the Vocabulary

The overriding principle in the exercises has been selectivity based upon thought and observation. Through your use of selectivity, you subconsciously employ your personal sense of style. Allowing selectivity to govern the choice of words you use means that you can create work that is confident, graphic, and informed.

By using the vocabulary when you are drawing, you are choosing the words to communicate with your audience. How you use the words is your choice, but the richer and more extensive your vocabulary, the richer your options of communication.

In this chapter we look at a range of styles and discuss how choices from the vocabulary have been used to create each unique image.

Opposite: *Evening Catwalk*, made with cut paper and pastel on Canson paper in 1986, is evidence of when I first began to see a sensibility emerge within my work. My interest in graphics, fashion, shape, and movement began to form a cohesive body of work that visually narrated my voice.

9.1 Using Shape

In this first set of drawings, we will look at how the use of shape can underpin any style of drawing. We were first introduced to the concept of shape in Chapter 3. Through the exercises in that chapter we began to understand why shape is essential to creating and seeing in terms of composition.

Whether incorporating line, texture, value, or color, thinking in terms of shape will allow you to recognize the elements of the composition and how to design those elements to great effect.

All of the illustrations accompanying this section are designed around the idea of shape. All are designed with a nod to selectivity and incorporate the compositional principle of repetition.

Below: This drawing incorporates contrasting shapes, each of which is exaggerated to complement the surrounding shapes. This is achieved by using the premise of opposition in the shape of the figures; the diagonals are also exaggerated to give a sense of movement to the silhouettes.

Selectivity was used in the choice of color and also in the use of negative shapes. The use of one-point perspective communicates depth, which is enhanced through the use of monochromatic color saturation from the foreground to the background figures.

Right: Selectivity is apparent in this illustration in the use of one large shape—the red gown. The minimal use of color creates a dramatic narrative, which is further enhanced by the additional premise of negative shapes. The loose brush stroke of the gown contrasts with the definite black silhouettes of the paparazzi that anchor and complement the figure.

9.1 Using Shape

Left: The simple shapes in this illustration of shoes use negative as well as positive shapes, while the asymmetrical design and use of diagonals give the composition a rhythmic movement.

Opposite: Here, one large black shape is used economically to frame the negative shapes of the figures. A static symmetrical layout is balanced by the rhythmic pattern of the windows of the cityscape. The figure on the left is composed of exaggerated straight lines, while its mirror on the right complements it with the use of curved lines.

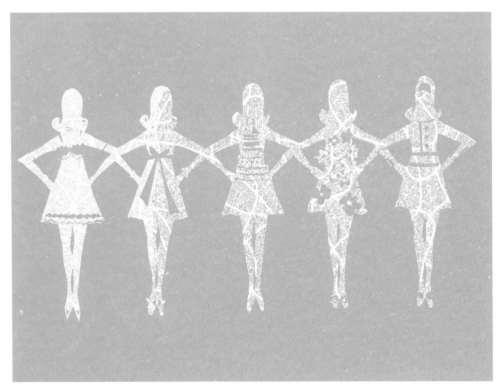

Left: Opposition and contrasting shapes are used in this illustration to break up the repetitious nature of the identical figures. The repeated pattern of the cut figures uses the negative shape to create variety.

9.2 Using Line

We started in Chapter 1 by looking at the integrity of line, while in Chapter 4 we explored different line qualities and their characters. We learned how line can be aloof or full of emotion, straight, curved, spontaneous, or studied and seemingly infinite in its ability to communicate anything and everything. Line is the immediate extension of the self and the pulse beneath the drawing.

Line should and will become an essential part of your visual vocabulary as an artist and illustrator.

In this section, all the images are based upon line and show how the selection of lines of different character from straight to studious can lend energy and expression to your style.

Below: The movement of the skaters is accentuated by the addition of exaggerated fluid lines on the figures' trailing scarves. The figures themselves are drawn in a contour line with the addition of a wash of color to form the illusion of a skirt.

Left: This illustration of geisha is created entirely with line—straight/curved, thin/thick, studious/continuous, and fluid.

Straight and curved lines define the form of the geisha, the structure of the umbrella, and the patterns gracing the kimonos. The floral hair accessories, the cherry blossoms in the fan, and some of the pattern on the kimonos are a combination of straight, curved, continuous, and studious lines. Some of the studious lines that form the hair are also used as a framing device to define the face. A variety of line quality, both thick and thin, is evident in the folds and form of the kimonos, nurturing an illusion of depth.

A thick fluid line moves diagonally in the foreground figure's kimono while a smaller, looser version is visible in the background figure's fan. The shape of the umbrella is a combination of straight and curved lines and is designed with a repetitive line pattern of a snowflake. The red shape that serves as a backdrop to the pattern is the only solid shape in the illustration.

177

Left: Here, fast energy lines are incorporated into a sketch of a fashion show. Overlapping contour lines are employed to give a feeling of movement to the audience. The models on the runway are drawn with a variety of line quality to emphasize depth and are complemented by the continuous thin line of the backdrop.

Opposite: Contour lines define the outline of the face and figures in this illustration. Studious lines examine the eyes, while flair lines of various weights overlap and flow throughout the hair. A large background composed of overlapping thick lines that form a pattern holds the figures. The addition of four contrasting black shapes subtly complements the various lines.

Right: This quick gesture drawing of the figure is composed entirely of lines. Four curved lines of various qualities and textures compose a shape that frames the face. A contour line describes the figure and helps to frame the negative shape of the face.

179

9.3 Using Shape and Line

As we have worked our way through the exercises in this book, and acquired an understanding of different words in the vocabulary, we have followed a progression from line, through shape, value, and composition. In this section we look at how shape can be used to complement line, and vice versa.

If shape is considered the soul of a dynamic composition then line pulsating through the work can be considered its heart. The combination is brilliant. Playing one off against the other is the start of a strong graphic illustration. Adding the capricious nature of line to shape can animate and energize what would otherwise be an interesting yet static illustration.

The illustrations in this section show that the use and balance of line, shape, and color in a drawing can make an arresting and dynamic image.

Opposite top: The addition of a washed shape within this illustration of the interior of St Patrick's Cathedral in New York creates the illusion of depth despite the use of contour line for the majority of the illustration. This illusion of depth is further nurtured by the use of shapes and line in white, which also illuminate the cathedral. The lines and shape work together to create an interesting balance without one monopolizing the other.

Opposite bottom: Lines of different characteristics overlap and blend against a static backdrop of solid shapes that serve to embellish the movement of the line.

Right: Fluid lines emanate off the gown of Sophia Loren in this illustration, entitled *Urgent*. The concept revolves around a gown that left a gold imprint on Ms Loren's co-star, Cary Grant, in the film *Houseboat*. The use of fluid line incorporates movement as well as the illusion of Ms Loren's ability to enchant. The addition of the dark static shapes complements the movement and direction of the lines.

Right: The composition of the shapes of the dogs and walkers are animated with the whimsical fluid lines of the leashes that dance between the shapes.

182

Above: Shape and line are blurred in this illustration of luncheon in the country and the city. The use of an identifiable contour line seems limited to the face and features. The rest of the elements in the illustration are a combination of line and shape and are sometimes indistinguishable from one another.

Right: Here the definite form and line of the figures are balanced by the use of colored shapes to fill in the shape of the gown. The shapes follow the direction of the lines and, as we saw in Chapter 8, decrease in saturation and repetition farther away from the viewer.

Chapter Ten
Breaking the Rules

All artistic disciplines are related. The process of making a work in the discipline of dance, music, literature, theater, or the visual arts is organic. It is an ever-changing state of movement and evolution. During the process, ideas not directly related to the current work will surface and can encourage a different line of thought or reason —a by-product of the initial idea, which can become the genesis of a new idea or direction for the artist to pursue. Artists with the foresight to recognize the value in the by-product generated by the initial idea will always have an edge in developing new work. These by-products are generated by accident, but the process of developing new work can also be engineered by the illustrator. This is the process we will explore in this chapter.

Illustration today necessitates that the artist not only be prolific but versatile. As an illustrator you may be called upon to create a mural or a textile pattern, design a book cover, webpage or site, storyboard a movie, or create an animation. Developing a strong, unique style will highlight and set your work apart from others. The upside is that this will guarantee you attention and exposure. The downside is that the style will eventually become dated and you will have become over-exposed or too well known as a practitioner of that one style.

As illustrators we are entertainers; we entertain the eye of the viewer and keep them engaged in the work. So, we need to come up with new tricks or styles that reinvent our vision and ideas to establish a new body of work. The ability to reinvent a style is an advantage that will prove invaluable during the course of your career.

Knowledge is power.

Opposite: Tobie Giddio embraces the idea that pushing the envelope is far more interesting than floating in one's comfort zone; one glance at her work is confirmation of that. Her ability to balance a graphic abstraction with an organic and Zen-like sensibility, as in this screenprint, *Beings*, creates work that is timeless and intriguing, with a beauty that leaves the viewer spellbound.

Breaking the Rules

Having completed the exercises in this book, you now understand the options and possibilities inherent in allowing the words of the vocabulary to influence your drawing and illustration. Knowing the rules, you can now break them; your personal vision, guided by thought, observation, and selectivity, will aid you in discarding what is not essential to that vision and retaining what will resonate in your work.

Having the confidence to break the rules is vital to your progression as an illustrator; breaking the rules is the genesis of reinventing your vision and style. Courage should be your constant companion when exploring new possibilities. They may provide the spark that leads you to a new style.

Break the Rules and Explore New Avenues

In order to reinvent your work, you need to first recognize what is your typical pattern or process of creating work. Everyone has a specific process; only when that process is reinvented will a new one emerge. So, recognize your pattern of making work and break it, mix it up, do the reverse, and explore other venues to recreate the process. Why not try some of the following?

If you draw with your right hand, why not switch to your left hand to examine the difference of the end result? This will also sharpen your use of the right hand.

If you always start a drawing at the top of the figure or visual, why not start at the bottom and work your way up? Or begin on the left side and work toward the right, or begin in the center and have the visual spiral out to the edges of the paper?

If you always begin with an exterior contour drawing, why not start by doing an internal drawing of value without line?

Why not create a drawing, rub it out, and create a new drawing from the history of the initial drawing?

Do a positive then a negative drawing.

Why not draw fast and furiously when you would usually draw slowly and vice versa?

Why not do a hundred small drawings in a day? Witness what will emerge when you begin to tire of your pattern and invent new solutions to accomplish the task.

Change your medium and color palette. Recognize which colors are most often used in your color palette, and use the complement of those colors to see what emerges.

If you always use gouache, use oil stick; if you use pastel, use watercolor; if you constantly use a dry medium, use a wet one.

Do a drawing or painting with a stick, twig, rock, sponge, or balsa wood.

If you always draw, then paint; if you always paint, sculpt or create a collage, lino-print, or woodcarving.

If you always draw on paper, draw on another surface; if you paint on canvas, paint on wood or vinyl.

If you always draw on white, why not draw on black?

If you always use neutral colors, switch to brights.

Place an assortment of colors nearby, close your eyes and select five colors to use.

Last but not least, remember that accidents are your best friends and darlings are your enemies. Allow accidents to occur, even encouraging an accident here and there. Use an accident to create an entirely new piece of work.

Darlings are those specializations that can become your trademark style. When the trademark becomes more prominent and begins to dictate the work then the work will become stale. Only by letting go of your darlings will you forward your work in a new direction.

In other words, break the rules, those self-imposed and those dictated by others. Do so confident in the knowledge that you have an informed choice; a choice that will forward your vision and success as an artist and illustrator.

Left and below: Study the compelling images of Daniel Egnéus and it is obvious that you are witnessing a successful marriage of life and art. Egnéus's versatility in drawing, painting, and architecture allows him to filter fantasy and personal concepts through a visual mixture of extreme perspective, fashion, and style. The images, which are always evolving, are stunning in execution, provocative in concept, and unforgettable.

Breaking the Rules

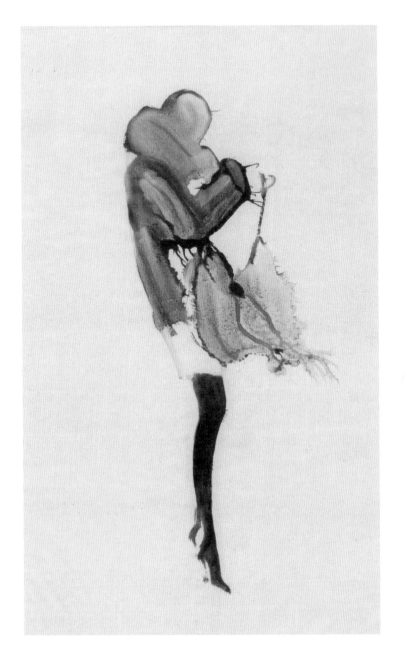

Above: Aurore de la Morinerie combines a
passion for art, fashion, nature, and culture to
execute fashion illustration images that are at
once economical, sophisticated, and luxurious.
De la Morinerie knows how to move paint,
whether through a brush or through the chance
of a monotype. A background in Chinese
calligraphy nurtures a confidence that allows her
to move beyond the usual notion of watercolor or
ink drawings to highlight the medium as muse.

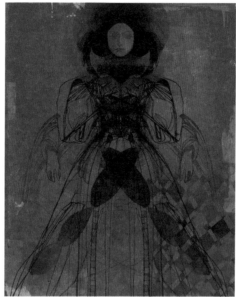

Left: Tina Berning's work blurs the boundaries between fine art and illustration through a mixture of ideas and use of media. Chance, accident, and emotion are incorporated easily into the work, as are paint, graphite, pastel, and collage. The end result elicits visuals that are always striking, expressive, unexpected, and fresh.

Below: To be a successful illustrator, one has to be prolific, curious, and a master of various styles and techniques. Carlos Aponte is all of the above, as evidenced by his extensive body of work, both figurative and graphic. Aponte's creative streak is not limited to his graphic concoctions. He is also an adept draftsman, a skill that is obvious in his fashion illustrations. A graphic sensibility underlies these three-dimensional images, sculpted from tape, which emerge through an orchestrated play of positive and negative shapes.

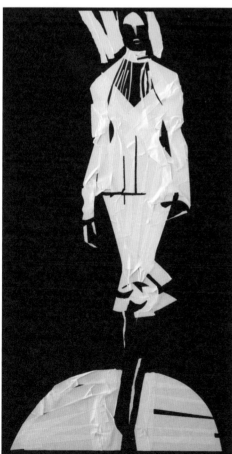

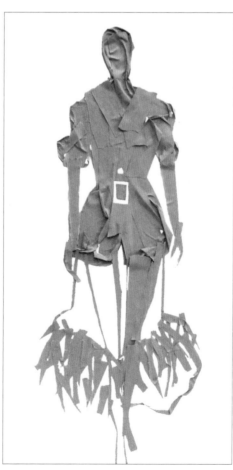

Glossary

Asymmetry Without symmetry, or any visible or implied balance. An asymmetrical illustration may well seem to have more going on to one side of the composition than the other.

Atmospheric perspective An illusion of recession created by depiction of atmospheric effects. As the distance between an object and the viewer increases, the contrast between the object and its background decreases. Its colors become less saturated and shift toward the background color.

Balancing-act method Drawing a figure in stages, starting from the left side, moving to the right, and then back to the left, and so on down the figure, using various points to anchor the line, without allowing one side to extend too far below the other. This method encourages the observation of differences between the right and left sides of the figure and helps ensure a drawing built on integrity.

Cold pressed paper Paper that has been cold pressed to achieve a slightly textured surface, often used for watercolors.

Conté crayon A drawing medium of compressed, powdered graphite or charcoal mixed with a wax or clay base, available in a range of colors, tones, and hardnesses, most effective on a tinted, rough paper.

Croquis From the French, croquer, "to sketch," a croquis is a rapid sketch of a model, often with loose drawing of clothes.

Gesso A primer, often white, that may be applied to a surface before painting in oil or acrylic to provide support and texture.

Gouache A heavier, opaque version of watercolor, containing more pigment and often an additional white pigment such as chalk, allowing quick coverage of substantial areas.

Gray scale A graduated representation of the different values of gray between black and white, broken down into a finite number of steps, usually ten, eleven, or twelve steps without color.

Hot pressed paper Paper with a fine-grained, smooth surface. It is appropriate for large washes of colour, and dries quickly.

Impressionism A movement that originated in France from the 1870s, which emphasized immediate visual impressions and the use of unmixed primary colors and small strokes to capture transient effects of light, often painted directly from nature.

Linear perspective A method for depicting the relations between the sizes of near and distant objects by making parallel lines converge at a vanishing point on the horizon.

Negative space Areas left empty once positive areas have been filled in by the artist.

Oil stick A combination of pigments, drying oils, and wax that creates an oil paint in a solid, crayon form.

Perspective A system that creates the illusion of three-dimensionality on a two-dimensional surface.

Positive space Where elements produce a figure or a field against a ground.

Rule of thirds A technique involving the division of a composition into three, both horizontally and vertically, and the positioning of key elements at the points where the lines intersect.

Scale Size relative to actual size, as in a scale model; size relative to human dimensions, as in small-scale or large-scale; to make larger or smaller.

Sumi-e painting A term for Japanese or Chinese ink-and-wash painting using ink dried and molded into sticks.

Symmetry Most commonly used to describe a mirror-like duplication (reflection) of elements on either side of a (frequently imaginary) central axis.

Value The gradation of tone from light to dark, irrespective of the color.

Vanishing point The point in linear perspective at which converging parallel lines appear to meet on the horizon line.

Vector graphics The use of geometrical lines and shapes, based on mathematical equations, to represent images in computer graphics.

Picture Credits

Further Reading

100 Ways to Paint People and Figures (How Did You Paint That?), North Light Books, Central Islip, NY, 2004

Adobe Creative Team, *Adobe Illustrator CS3: Classroom in a Book*, Adobe, Berkeley, CA, 2007

Adobe Creative Team, *Adobe Photoshop CS3: Classroom in a Book*, Adobe, Berkeley, CA, 2007

Atkinson, Jennifer, Holly Harrison, and Paula Grasdal, *Collage Sourcebook: Exploring the Art and Techniques of Collage*, Apple Press, Hove, 2004

Backmeyer, Sylvia (ed.), *Picture This: The Artist as Illustrator*, Central Saint Martins in association with The Herbert Press, London, 2005

Barnett, David, *Gary Hume, New Art Close Up*, Royal Jelly Factory, London, 2003

Baudot, François, *Gruau*, Editions Assouline, Paris, 2003

Blackman, Cally, *100 Years of Fashion Illustration*, Laurence King Publishing, London, 2007

Borrelli, Laird, *Fashion Illustration Now*, Thames and Hudson, London, 2000

Borrelli, Laird, *Stylishly Drawn*, Harry N. Abrams, New York, 2000

Borrelli, Laird, *Fashion Illustration Next*, Thames and Hudson, London, 2004

Brittain-Catlin, Timothy, Jane Audas, and Charles Stuckey, *The Cutting Edge of Wallpaper*, Black Dog Publishing, London, 2006

Bryant, Michele Wesen, *WWD Illustrated*, Fairchild, New York, 2004

CameraWork, *Unified Message In Fashion: Photography Meets Drawing*, Steidl Publishers, London, 2002

Caranicas, Paul and Laird Borrelli, *Antonio's People*, Thames and Hudson, London, 2004

Chapman, Noel and Carole Chester, *Careers in Fashion*, Kogan Page, London, 1999

Colchester, Chloë, *Textiles Today*, Thames and Hudson, London 2009

Cole, Bethan and Julie Verhoeven, *FatBottomedGirls 003*, Tdm Editions, Paris, 2002

Cole, Drusilla, *Patterns*, Laurence King Publishing, London, 2008

Colussy, Kathleen M. and Steve Greenberg, *Rendering Fashion, Fabric & Prints With Adobe Illustrator*, Prentice Hall, Upper Saddle River, NJ, 2006

Curtis, Brian, *Drawing From Observation: An Introduction to Perceptual Drawing* (second edition), McGraw-Hill, Boston, MA, 2009

Dawber, Martin, *Imagemakers: Cutting Edge Fashion Illustration*, Mitchell Beazley, London, 2004

Dawber, Martin, *The Big Book of Fashion Illustration*, Batsford, London, 2007

Delicatessen, *Fashionize: The Art of Fashion Illustration*, Gingko Press, Corte Madera, CF, 2004

Doonan, Simon, *Andy Warhol Fashion*, Chronicle Books, San Francisco, 2004

Ellwand, David, *Fairie-ality: The Fashion Collection*, Candlewick Press, Somerville, MA, 2002

Fletcher, Alan, *The Art of Looking Sideways*, Phaidon Press, London, 2001

Fogg, Marnie, *Print in Fashion*, Batsford, London, 2009

Genders, Carolyn, *Sources of Inspiration*, A&C Black, London, 2002

Hale, Robert Beverly, *Master Class in Figure Drawing*, Watson-Guptill Publications Inc., New York, 1991

Harrison, Hazel, *The Encyclopedia of Drawing Techniques*, Search Press Ltd, Tunbridge Wells, 2004

Harrison, Hazel, *The Encyclopedia of Watercolour Techniques: A Step-by-step Visual Directory, with an Inspirational Gallery of Finished Works*, Search Press Ltd, Tunbridge Wells, 2004

Hornung, David, *Colour: A Workshop for Artists and Designers*, Laurence King Publishing, London, 2004

Hyland, Angus and Roanne Bell, *Hand to Eye: Contemporary Illustration*, Laurence King Publishing, London, 2003

Klanten, Robert, *Illusive: Contemporary Illustration and its Context*, Die Gestalten Verlag, Berlin, 2005

Lhotka, Bonny et al., *Digital Art Studio: Techniques for Combining Inkjet Printing with Traditional Art Materials*, Watson-Guptill Publications Inc., New York, 2004

Lopez, Antonio, *60 70 80: Three Decades of Fashion Illustration*, Thames and Hudson, London, 1995

Mendelowitz, Daniel M., David L. Faber, and Duane A. Wakeham, *A Guide to Drawing* (seventh edition), Thomson Wadsworth, 2007

Morris, Bethan, *Fashion Illustrator*, Laurence King Publishing, London, 2007

New, Jennifer, *Drawing from Life: The Journal as Art*, Princeton Architectural Press, New York, 2005

Ocvirk, Otto G., Robert E. Stinson, Philip R. Wigg, Robert O. Bone, and David L. Cayton, *Art Fundamentals, Theory and Practice* (tenth edition), McGraw-Hill, Boston, MA, 2006

Ormont, Rhonda, *Career Solutions for Creative People*, Allworth Press, New York, 2004

Packer, William, *Fashion Drawing in Vogue*, Coward-McCann Inc., New York, 1983

Pao & Paws, *Clin D'Oeil: A New Look at Modern Illustration*, Gingko Press, Corte Madera, CF, 2004

Perrella, Lynne, *Artists' Journals and Sketchbooks: Exploring and Creating Personal Pages*, Rockport Publishers Inc., Rockport, MA, 2004

Perint Palmer, Gladys, *Fashion People*, Assouline, New York, 2003

Perry, Vicky, *Abstract Painting: Concepts and Techniques*, Watson-Guptill Publications Inc., New York, 2005

Raynes, John, *Figure Drawing and Anatomy for the Artist*, Octopus Books, London, 1979

Rees, Darrel, *How to be an Illustrator*, Laurence King Publishing, London, 2008

Shaw, Gwendolyn DuBois, *Seeing the Unspeakable: The Art of Kara Walker*, Duke University Press, Durham, NC, 2004

Simblet, Sarah, *The Drawing Book*, Dorling Kindersley, London, 2005

Smiley, Jan Bode, *Altered Board Book Basics and Beyond: For Creative Scrapbooks, Altered Books and Artful Journals*, C & T Publishing, Inc., Concord, CF, 2005

Smith, Paul, *You Can Find Inspiration in Everything*, Violette Editions, London, 2001

Steiner, Reinhard, *Egon Schiele, 1890–1918* (revised edition), Taschen, Cologne, 2000

Tallon, Kevin, *Digital Fashion Illustration*, Batsford, London, 2008

Weinmann, Elaine and Peter Lourekas, *Visual QuickStart Guide: Illustrator CS For Windows and Macintosh*, Peachpit Press, Berkeley, CA, 2004

Weinmann, Elaine and Peter Lourekas, *Visual QuickStart Guide: Photoshop CS For Windows and Macintosh*, Peachpit Press, Berkeley, CA, 2004

Williams, Robert A., *Illustration: Basics for Careers*, Prentice Hall, Upper Saddle River, NJ, 2003

Williams, Theo Stephen, *Streetwise Guide to Freelance Design and Illustration*, North Light Books, Central Islip, NY, 1998

Woods, Bridget, *Life Drawing*, The Crowood Press, Marlborough, 2003

Zahm, Volker (ed.), *Art Fashion: Original Works of Famous 20th Century Fashion Illustrators from the Collection Volker & Ingrid Zahm*, Zahm, Munich, 1994

Zeegen, Lawrence, *The Fundamentals of Illustration*, Ava Publishing, Lausannne, 2005

Zeegen, Lawrence, *Secrets of Digital Illustration*, RotoVision, Hove, 2007

Index